WHO *REALLY* WROTE THE BIBLE?

WHO *REALLY* WROTE THE BIBLE?

And Why It Should Be Taken Seriously Again

EYAL RAV-NOY and GIL WEINREICH

RICHARD VIGILANTE BOOKS

PUBLISHED BY RICHARD VIGILANTE BOOKS

Copyright © 2010 by

All Rights Reserved

www.richardvigilantebooks.com

RVB with the portrayal of a Labrador retriever in profile is a trademark
of Richard Vigilante Books

Book design by Charles Bork

Library of Congress Control Number: 2009911908

Applicable BISAC Codes:

REL006090RELIGION / Biblical Criticism & Interpretation / Old Testament

REL006050RELIGION / Biblical Commentary / General

ISBN 978-0-9800763-0-1

0-9800763-0-7

PRINTED IN THE UNITED STATES OF AMERICA

10 9 8 7 6 5 4 3 2 1

First Edition

to the Author

CONTENTS

PART I

Nonsense of Biblical Proportions

CHAPTER ONE

The New Secular Bible

Liberal religionists exploit the Bible to advance an agenda

On the Jewish holiday of Passover in 2001, the rabbi of Sinai Temple in Los Angeles, David Wolpe, gave a sermon. He told his congregants that the Exodus from Egypt they were commemorating most likely never occurred—at least not in the way described by the Bible.

One can only imagine the unease experienced by Rabbi Wolpe's congregants at this revelation. No Jewish holiday requires greater physical preparation and exertion: getting rid of all products with any kind of leavening; substituting special holiday dishes and utensils for regular tableware; thoroughly cleaning one's home, cars, and other properties; appointing an agent to sell one's bread and leavened products, etc.

All this effort and why? Because some ancient wise guys sitting in a smoke-filled cave made up some stories and had the chutzpah to embellish them with a not insignificant number of mandated religious rituals? Couldn't Rabbi Wolpe have made this announcement *before* all the holiday work had begun?

Just two years later, diagonally across the country, at St. Paul's Church in Concord, New Hampshire, local Episcopal church leaders chose Rev. V. Gene Robinson to be the first openly gay bishop. Whatever personal warmth one may feel for homosexual friends or acquaintances, most people's vision of a bishop, or any clergyman for that matter, would tend to exclude a non-celibate gay man as a religious role model.

These two little vignettes—the Exodus-denying rabbi and the Leviticus-denying priest—may seem unrelated. But both point to a society whose core religious values are up for grabs. Even though both incidents provoked a loud outcry from religious traditionalists, years later both men still have their jobs and arguably have greater influence and bigger platforms.

In 2008, *Newsweek* named Rabbi Wolpe America's number-one pulpit rabbi; two years earlier, Wolpe was seriously considered for the top position in the Conservative movement. (That same movement in December 2006 had its own election validating gay and lesbian rabbis and same-sex commitment ceremonies.) Reverend Robinson's career has also blossomed; he is arguably the most famous Episcopal bishop in America.

How have we gotten to the point where renowned leaders of the two Bible-based religions—and we could multiply the examples easily—can publicly take positions that *oppose* the Bible? The only possible answer is that they don't really *believe* in the Bible.

How did that happen? How did the Bible lose its authority? It was not an accident. It was the result of many or most of the spokesmen for the Bible religions adopting a specific set of ideas, quite recent in origin, about how, when, and by whom the Bible was written. It is true that most such religious leaders tend to be on the liberal side of things. But liberalism as such is not the problem. The problem is not bad ideology but bad Bible scholarship that has dominated now for more than one hundred years. To be sure, even without bad scholarship, people who want to deny the authority of the Bible will find a way. But with the scholars on their side, armed with elaborate theories of multiple authorship and sources, phantom editors, and later interpolations, Wolpe, Robinson, and liberal religionists like them can have it both ways. They can profess, as they do, to revere the Bible, but then find wiggle room to depart from any particular passage they don't like. Free from its strictures, liberal religionists can exploit this new secular Bible to advance an agenda, cloaking their own preferences in the garments of religious authority and tradition.

What separates evangelical Christians, Roman Catholic traditionalists, and Orthodox Jews from their liberal religious cousins is a belief that the Bible* is the word of God. If the Creator of the world thought to record His views in a book for us, then it speaks with authority, its demands are obligatory, and to read that book is to know the mind of God.

If the Bible is not the word of God, then its words can and ultimately will be used to mean whatever people want them to— or they will simply be ignored. In our time, the most powerful excuse for exploiting the Bible, rather than taking it seriously, is a school of biblical scholarship that denies that the Bible was written by a single author. As we will show, this "scholarship" is not only flawed but actually makes the Bible much harder to read and understand.

A fundamental principle of Judaism is that of *Torah MiSinai*: God gave the Torah to the Jewish people at Sinai. For all the challenges that liberal religionists, whether Jewish or Christian, throw out about modern archeology (e.g., Wolpe's claim that the Exodus did not occur), modern biology (i.e., that the theory of evolution is at odds with the biblical account of creation), and so forth, a

---

* Throughout this book we use the term "Bible" because of its wide acceptance in English. However, unless otherwise indicated, all references to the Bible in this book are meant to refer just to its first five books, also known as the Torah or Pentateuch.

simple question can be asked: if the Bible is not true, then why be religious? Secular intellectuals are far more consistent and far more rational than believers in liberal religion.

As commentator Dennis Prager wrote in response to Rabbi Wolpe's Passover sermon in 2001, "If the Exodus did not occur, there is no Judaism."[1] Almost everything in the Hebrew Bible and Jewish liturgy is pinned to the twin notions that God created the world and that He intervened in history to free the Jewish people from Egyptian bondage. No other people did or would claim to be descendants of despised slaves nor would they maintain as its founding document a Bible that disparages the Jewish people as ingrates, rebels, and complainers and that accords hero status to non-nationals such as Pharaoh's daughter, who saved Moses; Jethro, who teaches his son-in-law Moses how to govern; or Moses himself, who was raised as an Egyptian.

Many other details, such as names, place names, and archeological findings are consistent with the biblical account, and the fact that a widely dispersed nation has relayed this unflattering story from generation to generation (in the same way, whether in Poland or in Yemen) is testimony to the power of this formative historical experience.

Unlike believers in the biblical account of the Exodus or rational skeptics in the secular world, liberal religionists deny the truth of the Bible yet still observe onerous religious practices. Why is this? Among regular folks, the reason may be that, at some level, religious practice gives meaning to their lives.

But among movement leaders, another reason comes to mind. The Bible has tremendous legitimizing force. Rather than do away with such a powerful tool, liberal religious leaders want to update it to confer respect upon contemporary pet causes. Today's popular causes in liberal circles include environmentalism, multiculturalism, feminism, and pacifism. A classic example of this kind of issue advocacy is commonly seen among rabbis, priests and ministers who oppose capital punishment.

These death penalty opponents, who cite (and mistranslate) the sixth of the Ten Commandments as "Do not kill," are bad Bible scholars. The text actually says, "Do not murder." That is to say, taking the life of an innocent person is fundamentally morally different from putting a guilty murderer to death. In fact, the commandment to execute murderers is seen as so fundamental to justice that it is the second commandment given in the Torah (after "Be fruitful and multiply"); it applies to all of humanity (i.e., it was first given to Noah, the father of all mankind); and it is the only commandment that is repeated in each one of the five books of the Torah.[2]

Instances of liberal religionists misusing their spiritual mantle run the entire spectrum of causes, from social issues to foreign affairs. Nowadays, liberal Bible thumpers urge Israel to give up land to neighbors at war with them, whereas the Bible is explicit that God gave the Land of Israel to the Jewish people and wanted to evict Molech worshippers. (Molech was worshipped through child sacrifice; today's Palestinians routinely sacrifice children, using them as human shields, indoctrinating them into jihad, and strapping suicide belts on them.) The more things change, the more they remain the same.

CHAPTER TWO

The New Secular Gods

A fragmented Bible reduces God to caricature

C ould a vast multinational group of leading scholars with credentials from the finest academic institutions all be wrong?

Yes, and for the most obvious of reasons. Most scholars and intellectuals, no matter how careful and precise they are with any particular piece of scripture, operate within the dominant paradigm, the orthodoxy, of their time. The more universally accepted the background assumptions of any discipline, the less likely they are to be questioned. Within the parameters of the orthodoxy, debate may be fierce, but those who actually challenge the orthodoxy are excluded from the debate and dismissed as cranks.

The reigning orthodoxy in academic Bible studies is known as the "documentary hypothesis." It posits that the Bible is a composite of various ancient documents that someone at a later date redacted into the work we know today as the Bible's first five books. Though the documentary hypothesis is the bedrock of "modern" biblical scholarship, it is nearly three hundred years old.

Early Bible skeptics included the Englishman Thomas Hobbes and the Dutch Jew Benedictus Spinoza.[1] Hobbes's *Leviathan* (1651) pointed to seemingly anachronistic language in the Bible as internal evidence of its later authorship. Spinoza asserted that the Bible was primarily the work of a later historian, most likely Ezra the Scribe.[2] Both denied Mosaic authorship based on references to Moses in the third person, the narration of his death, and most especially the recording of events after his death.[3]

But the real turning point in Western critical analysis came a century later with the publication in 1753 of the work of Jean Astruc,[4] a French physician and amateur biblical exegete. Astruc is known as the "Father of the Documentary Hypothesis" because he pointed out that the Bible might be a composite made up of at least two different sources. His basis for this claim derived from the simple but arresting observation that the books of Genesis and Exodus (his dissertation concerned only these two books) constantly alternate between two distinct Divine names.

Sometimes the Bible uses the Four-Letter-Name (a transliteration of the Hebrew letters י-ה-ו-ה or Y-H-W-H) that is usually rendered as Jeho-vah or "the Lord" in English and is conventionally referred to by Jews as "Hashem," meaning "the Name."[5] And sometimes the Bible uses "Elokim,"[6] which is translated as "God." These Bible segments would later be referred to as the J source (for Jeho-vah) and the E source (for Elokim), respectively.[7]

Astruc also observed "doublets"—what he took to be the Bible's two versions of Creation stories; two versions of the Flood; and two versions of the various stories involving the patriarchs. He found that these doublets often exactly corresponded to the alternate uses of the Divine name. For example, the so-called "first account" of creation in Genesis 1 uses the name Elokim thirty-five times, whereas the "second account" found in Genesis 2 uses Hashem-Elokim eleven times. But Genesis 1 never uses the name Hashem and Genesis 2 never uses just Elokim.[8]

As the nineteenth century dawned, the literary unity of the Bible seemed to unravel further. Mainly German academic critics[9] doubled the number of biblical source texts from two to four by following the same logic as their predecessors. Whereas the E source had initially appeared as a unity because of its use of the Divine name Elokim, it had doublets of its own within which these scholars discovered differences of style, language, and interests. Because this newly exposed strand exhibited a strong interest in priests and in ritual matters, that document came to be known as the Priestly source, or P.[10]

Next, the Bible critics posited that Deuteronomy contained what they assumed were doublets of stories found in the other four books of the Bible, most notably in its differently worded version of the Ten Commandments. The nineteenth-century Bible critic Wilhelm M. L. de Wette cited the story of manna falling from heaven as an example of the simple and unselfconscious style of the first four books that contrasts with the didactic preaching of Deuteronomy. Whereas in Exodus manna is a miracle uncommented upon by the author, in Deuteronomy it is an object lesson: "Man does not live on bread alone, but . . . on whatever the Lord decrees."[11] Thus the Bible critics found the fourth source of the Bible, D.

Academic critics throughout the nineteenth century hypothesized that various fragments, supplements, or documents had been enlarged or joined in some way by an editor seeking to preserve elements of the multiple Bibles considered sacred by important constituencies. The result was a heavily redacted and at times redundant and contradictory text. It was the German academic Julius Wellhausen who in 1878 fully developed and popularized this theory of multiple authorship.

Wellhausen claimed to identify four major documents, each

with a complex literary history of its own. The earliest, supposedly, was the J document, and then E, both composed during
the era of the first kings of Israel (about a millennium after the
Bible's Exodus account); these two documents were merged into a
single J–E text. Later came D, the author of Deuteronomy, which
was said to have been written at the time of King Josiah. Lastly,
according to Wellhausen—but disputed by modern Bible critics,
who maintain that P preceded D—came the P document, which
was written at the time of the Second Temple. The editor of the
final composite Bible was called R, for Redactor. This hypothesis, with some revisions and updates, has become the orthodoxy
governing Bible scholarship in academia and liberal theological
seminaries today.

Let us look at a classic example. The Bible critics have long
observed that the Bible contains two apparently contradictory creation stories: a "first account" in Genesis 1, and a "second account"
in Genesis 2 and 3.[12]

The first account, allegedly authored by P, uses the name
Elokim for God. It does not report intimate conversations
between God and man, but only general commands portraying
God as transcendent. This is apparent from the process of creation, which is cold, methodical (day by day), impersonal, and
domineering (God commands and the world obeys). This first
account can be seen as a metaphysical treatise dealing with the
question of existence and origins. But it has no moral story to
tell, no specific command to mankind, and no stories of angels
or talking snakes.

All of these elements are, however, found in the second
account, which uses the name Hashem for God. This version,
allegedly authored by J, is more intimate; its language is more
flowery; and it deals with human issues such as sin and its consequences, freedom of choice, and man's nearness to God.

THE BIBLE CRITICS' TWO ACCOUNTS OF CREATION		
DIFFERENCES	1ST ACCOUNT GENESIS 1 (P)	2ND ACCOUNT GENESIS 2 (J)
Name of God	God is called Elokim	God is called Hashem
Nature of God	God is transcendent. There are no conversations with God	God is immanent. Man converses with God
Creation	Creation is methodical (day by day), impersonal, and domineering	Creation is haphazard, improvised, and personal
Motif	Philosophical	Mythical (talking snakes, etc.)
Order of Creation	Plant life, then animal life, then man and woman simultaneously	Man, then plant life, then animals, and finally woman
Language of Creation	Creates (*bara* in Hebrew)	Forms (*yatzar* in Hebrew)
Nature of Man	Pinnacle of creation	Human and flawed

Thus deconstructed, the Bible critics' Bible is host to two competing concepts of God. P's god is Aristotelian. He is a detached creator following a scientific method. J's god is no scientist; he's a humanities major. He's a "people person" for whom morality, rebuke, and punishment are consuming questions.

Also, the two gods seem to create their world in two different ways. P's god "creates" (Hebrew verb: *bara*) by "speaking." J's god is "hands-on": he "forms" man (Hebrew verb: *yatzar*) and "plants" a garden.

The two gods are at odds on the sequence of creation. In P's account of creation, God creates plant life, then animal life, then man and woman simultaneously. In J's account of creation, God first creates man, then plant life, animals next, and finally woman.

Finally, the two gods have different views of man. P's god is removed, and J's is deeply involved. For P's god, man is the dignified, final creative act of God. For J, man is the childlike creature in the garden, fearing punishment. P's god blesses man and endows his noble creation with lordship over the earth, whereas J's god orders man not to snack on the fruit of the Tree of Knowledge.

P's god, though aloof, is not hard to please; on each day of creation, P tells us, "And God saw that it was good." J's moralizing god sees the darker side of man: "And Hashem saw that the wickedness of Man was great upon the earth, and that every product of the thoughts of his heart was but evil always." (Genesis 6:5)

Split the opening narrative of Genesis into two accounts and the result really is two different gods. That is about as dramatic a contradiction as there could be in a book whose purpose is to reveal God to man. Two different gods implies two different religions. It must mean that the whole biblical account is unreliable and probably fictional.

When a young student or religious seminarian hears his professor or clergyman say, "Did you know the Bible has two different accounts of creation?"—his belief in the credibility of the Bible may be instantly extinguished (if he's not wise enough to question his teacher). If the Bible includes two different accounts of creation, that necessarily means that at least one account is untrue.

As we'll see in the next chapter, the four-author hypothesis is unsupportable. In the meantime, notice how the notion of multiple gods plays out in our world. P's Aristotelian, deist god is echoed in the "man is good" worldview that informs secular humanism and the idea of man as an essentially noble creature not in need of a repressive biblical moral code.

Likewise, J's hypercritical bully god who plays hide and seek with man in the Garden of Eden parallels the "man is sinful" viewpoint that has been rapidly depleting Christian church pews with every passing generation. If people liked being told that they were going to hell, Noah's ark would have had many more passengers. Blindness to our own faults and a disposition to think well of ourselves make this message a turn-off.

Bible critics, intellectuals, and dour churchmen have all had a hand in undermining the Bible through their selective readings.

But there is another way. One can read the Bible as a coherent, unified narrative that offers a perspective on the world's creation *and* a philosophy of good and evil. In this united Bible, God is the creator of the world *and* He cares about his creation. Not only is this view more uplifting than the alternatives, it turns out that the "naïve" believers in a single author of the Bible are better scholars and far more up to date than the believers in the reigning orthodoxy.

CHAPTER THREE

Maverick Ministers

Why believers in the same Bible espouse contradictory views

On September 11, 2001, just yards away from Ground
Zero, Dr. Rowan Williams, the future archbishop of
Canterbury, was in New York City at a conference
on spirituality. In the immediate aftermath of the terrorist attacks,
Williams wrote a book, *Writing in the Dust: After September 11,*[1] in
which he called for understanding and argued against retaliation.
"If I decide to answer in the same terms, that is how the conversa-
tion will continue," Williams wrote.

"We have something of the freedom to consider whether or
not we turn to violence and so . . . are rather different from those
who experience their world as leaving no other option." Williams
discouraged harsh rhetoric about the terrorists: "Bombast about
evil individuals doesn't help in understanding anything."

Just a few days later one could hear quite a bit of bombast
directed not against the terrorists but against their victims at the
Trinity United Church of Christ on Chicago's south side. On the
first Sunday after 9/11, the Reverend Jeremiah Wright justified
this unprovoked attack on his countrymen as a deserved and long-
delayed retaliation for a catalog of American crimes:

We bombed Hiroshima, we bombed Nagasaki, and we

nuked far more than the thousands in New York and the Pentagon, and we never batted an eye.

"We have supported state terrorism against the Palestinians and black South Africans, and now we are indignant because the stuff we have done overseas is now brought right back to our own front yards. America's chickens are coming home to roost,"[2] he told his congregation.

So days after al-Qaeda set three thousand innocent Americans ablaze in a then-unimaginable act of terrorism, we have two church leaders who seem to sympathize with mass murderers. Even so, their approaches are starkly different. Archbishop Williams wants us to understand the terrorists, specifically why they had no other choice, and does not want to fight back. Rev. Wright implies there should be yet more violence—that America has not been punished nearly enough.

Williams is a pacifistic, self-hating Westerner (in 2008 he declared that the rule of Shariah, Islamic religious law, in the United Kingdom should not be resisted), and Wright is a militant black nationalist who seems to rejoice in the humiliation of the United States. Two very different men. But though they are both Christian ministers, they also seem to have two different gods: one, an angry punisher; the other, a turn-the-other-cheek pacifist. Under the "modern" method of reading the Bible, they are entitled: every Christian and every Jew gets to pick.

God of Judgment, God of Mercy

In the last chapter, we saw how the Bible critics divided up the Bible based on Astruc's eighteenth-century observation that the two Divine names, Hashem and Elokim, line up with different personalities, literary styles, and conceptions of God.

But tearing the Bible into shreds—tearing any well-constructed book into shreds—yields a plethora of incomplete, superficial, and inherently contradictory pictures.

Suppose someone wrote a fascinating book about you, a book so great and rich that it was revered by every civilization exposed to it. Naturally the book portrays the many aspects of your personality: your intelligence, your wit, your love of music. Then one day a professor announces that actually this is a biography of three different people—a smart guy, a funny guy, and a musician—conflated by some ancient editor. What is the result? Instead of one great story featuring your fascinating, complex self, thanks to the professor we now have three uninteresting cardboard characters that do not accurately reflect your character but behave in tediously predictable ways.

Let's take a well-known biblical image from Genesis as an example of how the Bible critics denude the Bible of its literary power. The critics ascribe to J the story of man's expulsion from the Garden of Eden, which is left guarded by the Cherubim (angels) with the flame of the ever-turning sword—a paradise lost to which we never again return. Or is it? Actually, the Cherubim do reappear in the book of Exodus—in a section ascribed to P—where they form a part of the cover of the Ark of the Covenant, which houses the tablets containing the Ten Commandments.

So while the Cherubim protect the Tree of Life in J's version of Genesis, they protect the Torah in P's version of Exodus. Reading the two stories together, the message is clear: the Torah is a Tree of Life, and if we want access to the Garden of Eden, it is to be found through the Torah, i.e., following God's commandments.

While the Cherubim are not mentioned again in the Torah, they are hinted at in a passage in Deuteronomy that uses language parallel to the story of the expulsion from Eden. Compare the texts:

THE GARDEN OF EDEN	THE LAND OF ISRAEL
J	D
"And having driven the man (*vaygaresh*)**, He stationed** (*vayashken*—literally: caused to dwell) **at the east of the Garden of Eden the Cherubim . . . to guard the path to the Tree of Life."** (Genesis 3:24)	"He drove (*vaygaresh*) the enemy away from before you, and He said: 'Destroy!' Thus Israel shall dwell (*vayishkon*) secure. . . ." (Deuteronomy 33:27–28)[3]

This is a classical biblical bookend. In Genesis, in the beginning of the Torah, God drives man out of the garden, and his exile east of Eden is enforced by the Cherubim stationed (literally, caused to dwell) there. Just as Adam stood gazing from the east into the Garden of Eden from which he was exiled, in Deuteronomy, at the end of the Torah, the Is raelites stand immediately to the east of their promised land. Here God promises to drive the Israelites' enemy away, and having received their Torah, they can now enter the land and dwell there securely.

The Bible critics—in dividing up the Bible—rob the story of its impact. The critics give the expulsion story to J, for whom the Garden of Eden is seen as a mythical idea to which we lack access. P (whose Cherubim guard the Tabernacle's Ark of the Covenant) says that the most essential thing is the Temple, the center of religious authority. D's Eden is the state, since only superior power can allow Israel to dwell securely.

WHERE CHERUBIM DWELL		
J	P	D
Cherubim guard the Garden of Eden	Cherubim guard the Ark of the Covenant	Hints to Eden— but points to the Promised Land

In other words, J is trying to sell us on fairy tales; P is forcing religion down our throats; and D's perspective seems to be that power is the only language that is understood in the Middle East. The truth is that all three are important: genuine power, proper religious authority, and the right theological symbolism.

These lessons are relevant to all nations that claim a biblical heritage, such as the United States and Israel. Following the Bible's guidelines, they should strive to possess superior military power to defend against enemies; they require laws and institutions that will maintain a moral order within society; and they need individual religious strivers with a sense of moral accountability.

Taken apart, J, P, and D offer narrow and competing worldviews. But taken together, as the Bible was meant to be, these episodes are about the destiny of man. They're about truth, not myth. They're about how to have a just society, good laws, power to promote good in the world, how to live a happy and peaceful life, and so on.

Does your priest, minister, or rabbi see the Bible as multi-dimensional or mono-dimensional? Is the Bible profound and instructive, or insipid and unconvincing? In the next chapter, we explain how the Bible critics not only are not, but can not be right.

CHAPTER FOUR

Criticizing the Critics

The fatal flaws in their hypothesis

People who take the Bible seriously are going to ask questions. Critical questioning of the Bible does not imply hostility to a work held sacred by religious believers. Rather, such questioning should be encouraged as a means of deepening our understanding of the text.

We argue that most contemporary biblical criticism is a fraud, an exercise in futility, and a model of lemming-like conformity. On balance, the academic study of the Bible has *not* contributed to a better understanding of the text. Rather, the field seems to be devoted to the circular task of proving itself correct.

An excellent example of this closed circle is a statement by one of the field's most prominent spokesmen, Richard Elliott Friedman, who, in his popular book—*Who Wrote the Bible?*—dismisses opposing views in a single sentence: "At present, however, there is hardly a biblical scholar in the world actively working on the problem who would claim that the Five Books of Moses were written by Moses—or by any one person."[1]

A condescending footnote adds insult to injury: "There are many persons who claim to be biblical scholars. I refer to scholars who have the necessary training in languages, biblical archeology, and literary and historical skills to work on the problem, and who meet, discuss, and debate their ideas and research with other scholars through scholarly journals, conferences, etc."[2]

Despite this rather pompous dismissal of any dissent, it is the academic critics of the single authorship of the Bible who are short on objective evidence, and it is the documentary hypothesis that is unscholarly and cannot withstand logical scrutiny.

Imaginary Scrolls and Fabricated History

Our argument begins with the total absence of any physical evidence that the J, E, P, or D documents ever existed. Centuries of archeological discoveries have turned up ancient Torah scrolls and fragments, but none have been at odds with the Torah familiar to all Bible readers.

It should be emphasized that Jewish tradition stringently forbids the destruction of a Torah scroll. If a Torah scroll is no longer fit for use because even a single letter is hand-formed incorrectly or the scroll is beyond repair, the Torah is ritually and respectfully interred, as a deceased person would be. Hence, there are countless Torah scrolls, many of which were laid to rest in near-perfect condition, that await discovery in a Middle Eastern cave or manuscript burial site (called a *genizah*). Of the numerous finds to date, not a single one is a pre-redacted J, E, P, or D scroll, document, or fragment.

The absence of such scrolls from the archeological record does not by itself prove they do not exist. But it should make the Bible critics exceedingly cautious in upholding a belief for which there is not a scrap of tangible support.

Facts are stubborn, and so are Jews

In addition to the lack of physical evidence, there is a common-sense objection to the documentary hypothesis. The idea that ancient Israelites with different traditions would agree to unite their sacred texts (e.g., an early J text with, say, an early E text) would appear strongly at odds with the disputatious nature of the Jewish people. As the old Jewish saying goes, if you've got two Jews, you've got three opinions.

Indeed, it's not for nothing that the oldest record we have about the Jewish people, the Bible itself, describes Jews as "a stiff-necked people." This unyielding national characteristic does not square with the accommodating approach assumed by the documentary hypothesis, though it may help explain why the Jewish people have been able to survive throughout the millennia despite unceasing existential threats.

Fiction over Facts

To support their theory of multiple authorship, the Bible critics also have their own version of the history of Israel. But the evidence for their version of history is as nonexistent as any scroll fragments reflecting the various alphabet of authors.

In this view, the crucial historical turning point in Israelite history was the division of the united Jewish monarchy after the reign of King Solomon in the tenth century BCE. The Bible critics speculate that the political split produced rival priesthoods, with one set of "Aaronid" priests (descendants of Aaron) centered on Jerusalem in the southern kingdom of Judah and another set of "Mushite" priests (descendants of Moses) based in the priestly city of Shilo in the northern kingdom of Israel. The critics claim that each group of priests wrote down its remembered traditions in its own sacred scrolls: the book of J for the Aaronid priests based in the south; the book of E for the Shilo Mushite priests based in the north.

This alleged rivalry between Shilo priests and Aaronid priests is not recorded in the Bible or supported anywhere else. There are indeed, until this very day, known descendants of Aaron, often with the last name Cohen or Kohan; not only family tradition but also modern genetics supports this notion. But there is no historical or textual evidence to back up the idea that priests in Shilo defined themselves as descendants of Moses, much less as rivals of the descendants of Aaron.[3]

The Bible critics extend their historical fiction to the late eighth century BCE, claiming that the Aaronid priests wrote a new book—the P text—to strengthen priestly prerogatives in temple worship. The Bible critics then add that a century later a Shilo scribe wrote a restatement of the law (Deuteronomy) that would support King Josiah's political reforms.

The critics' histories are meant to show that the biblical source documents have strong political biases: that J and P were pro-Aaron texts and E and D were pro-Moses texts. The critics say that during times of political upheaval, the J and E texts were merged; P later incorporated J–E into a pro-Aaron master text; later still, in the time of Ezra (whom the Bible records as a descendant of Aaron), the redactor (some Bible critics finger Ezra himself) cobbled J, E, P, and D into what we today call the Bible.

Apart from the fact that this is all historically baseless, to believe that partisans of any of the alleged predecessor Bibles would agree to lay their differences aside and create a hybrid document is as plausible as today's Jews all coalescing around religious Orthodoxy or non-Orthodoxy, Ashkenazi customs or Sephardic ones, a hawkish policy for the State of Israel or a dovish one, Republican policies or Democratic ones.

The Narrative Gap

Besides the lack of physical and historical evidence and the implausibility of stiff-necked Jews papering over their deepest differences, the flaws in the documentary hypothesis go far deeper. The Bible critics' theory of multiple authorship leaves ubiquitous gaping holes in the Bible narrative. In J, Moses is sent to Egypt to take the Israelites out. In the next scene, the Israelites are outside of Egypt. What happened to the plagues? Did J somehow know that E and P would explain the process of the Exodus years later?

And did J know that someday P would explain how Noah built his ark, thus allowing J to omit it completely from his part of the story of Noah's ark?

In J, Joseph is sold as a slave. The next thing we know, he is running the Egyptian economy as viceroy of Egypt. One has to read E to fill in the missing drama.

And how did J get the preposterous notion that Pharaoh ordered all newborn boys, including Egyptian ones, to be put to death?

P opens the Bible using the name Elokim, but by the book of Exodus he is primarily using J's name, Hashem. Only in P do Abram and Sarai get their new names, Abraham and Sarah, yet J and E somehow knew about it and use those names ever after. J gives Jacob five of his twelve sons (Reuben being one of them); E gives him seven more sons and a daughter (Reuben *not* being one of them).

A reader must suppose that the patriarch Jacob had twelve sons and a daughter by adding J's narrative to E's. In reality, however, the text does not cooperate with this approach because there is an unexpected cameo appearance by one of the sons that J introduced (Reuben, when he brings his mother, Leah, mandrakes) in an E text. The problems are literally endless.

E tells us that Sarah proclaims that all her friends are happy for her, neglecting to inform us that Sarah's son Isaac has been born; that information was supposedly supplied by P, who allegedly lived after E.

And a personal favorite: In E, Moses makes his first appearance in Midian, tending Jethro's flocks. Who is this Moses? Is he a Midianite?[4]

The argument that an editor, R, put this all together ignores the fact that the Bible narrative is constantly building on earlier passages. Readers never catch J *not* knowing something that P mentioned earlier, as one would expect if the Bible were truly such a complex composite.

Either J, E, P, and D had substantially the same stories, and R didn't have these difficult narrative gaps to smooth over, in which case why and on what basis would anyone suspect that there were multiple authors in the first place? Or, we accept the narrative gaps, and somehow the distinct strands from authors living at different times all just came together coherently. Very much like Shakespeare and Mark Twain's great collaboration, *Hamletberry Finn*.

So how does a Bible critic deal with the following gaping narrative hole? E's very first contribution to the Bible was a passage found in Genesis 20. That's right, twenty chapters into the book. Did E skip Bible class for the first few years of his life, or did he simply not think that the Creation, the Flood, and Abraham were worthy of being mentioned in his version of the Bible?

This is how Richard Elliott Friedman excuses E:

"The author of J was more interested in the patriarchal period while the author of E was more focused on the Exodus and wilderness age."[5]

This is nothing short of academic arrogance. Neither Friedman nor any Bible critic ever met E, ever interviewed E, or ever saw a manuscript with E's signature on it. All we know about E ultimately derives from the fact that the Bible critics have assigned to him large parts of Exodus as well as portions set in the wilderness age. E may be like the emperor sporting his new clothes. Some German academic "discovered" him, and generations of successors flattered their professors by saying they "see" him too. Overstatements of the kind cited above go far beyond the kind of caution one would expect from a scholar.

The fact that no J, E, P, or D documents exist should give you pause. The implausibility of Jews getting together and cutting and pasting their sacred documents should cause you to question the documentary hypothesis. The more extravagant claims about the personal interests of individuals who left no written self-referential traces should make you dubious. The narrative gaps that exist based on the Bible critics' division of sources strain credulity. And all of this makes one wonder how the documentary hypothesis ever got off the ground to begin with. In the next chapter, we reveal that, despite the scholarly attention it has received, the documentary "hypothesis" never amounted to a real hypothesis at all.

CHAPTER FIVE

The Bible Critics' Name Game

Do they even believe their own hypothesis?

Ask any Bible critic or clergyman who accepts the multiple authorship hypothesis to state just one proof to support his view of multiple authorship of the Bible. Almost certainly he will answer that the Bible uses different names for God: for example, "Elokim" is used in Genesis 1, the first account of creation (supposedly written by P); and "Hashem" is used in Genesis 2–3, the second account of creation (supposedly written by J). Although most Bible critics will begin with this argument, the truth is that not even they believe in its validity.

Let's conduct a simple thought experiment. Let's assume for argument's sake that it was Moses who wrote the first five books of the Bible. We begin flipping through his book, and, as intelligent readers, we are struck with a question: "Why does Moses refer to God as Elokim at times and at other times as Hashem?"

Two possibilities come to mind:

1. Moses didn't care which name he used. He had two names of God at his disposal, and he arbitrarily chose to use Elokim here and Hashem there. Or:

2. Moses had a very good reason. Unfortunately we don't know the reason, but if we could ask him, he would gladly tell us what he was thinking.

Both of these options agree on one point: it is OK for one author to use two different names for God.

Enter the Bible critics proposing a novel third explanation: Maybe it wasn't really Moses who wrote the Bible. Perhaps the two names of God indicate that at least two people wrote the Bible, maybe three: J, E, and P.

To this the intelligent Bible reader would immediately respond with a simple question for the Bible critic: "According to your theory, could P use two different names for God (Elokim and Hashem)?"

This would be a moment of truth for the Bible critic. He could have only one of two responses:

1. No. P, E, and J would never use different names; otherwise we would have to apportion their texts to two Js, two Es, and two Ps. Or:

2. Yes. P, E, and J may indeed use different names for God, and for two reasons. Either they didn't care which name they used—they had two names for God at their disposal, and they arbitrarily chose to use Elokim here, Hashem there—*or* they could answer that they had a very good reason why they used different names for God. Unfortunately we don't know why, but if we could ask them, they would gladly tell us what they were thinking.

The Bible critics make the latter choice. They know, and have always known, that J, E, and P all alternate between the names Elokim and Hashem. This fact does not cause them to split J in two, E in two, or P in two. Rather, the Bible critics assume that their authors knew both Divine names and used them either arbitrarily (option 1) or purposefully (option 2).

But if that were the case, why couldn't Moses have alternated between the two Divine names—either arbitrarily or purposefully? This logic alone is enough to collapse the entire documentary hypothesis. Nay, our analysis shows that a working hypothesis never existed in the first place.

Are P and E Schizophrenic?

The Names of God argument does not and never did have any explanatory power for this simple reason: J, E, and P show no more consistency in the use of God's name than Moses does.

Consider that P—who is above all famous for his authorship of the entire book of Leviticus—almost exclusively uses the name Hashem (*about three hundred times*), and almost never the name Elokim (*only five times*), in that entire book. And yet the Bible critics tell us that P got his start in Genesis 1, the Creation story, where he only uses the name Elokim. If P is allowed to use two names in a single document, or to use one name predominantly in one document and a different name exclusively in another, why is Moses or the original author not allowed to do the same?

This same line of reasoning goes for E. Consider the following two verses that the Bible critics claim were written by E in their entirety:

Jethro, priest of Midian, Moses' father-in-law, heard all that ELOKIM had done for Moses and for Israel His people, how HASHEM had brought Israel out from Egypt. (Exodus 18:1)

. . . And Moses went up to ELOKIM. HASHEM called to him from the mountain, saying, "Thus shall you say to the house of Jacob and declare to the children of Israel . . ." (Exodus 19:3)

Here E is caught using both Divine names in a single verse. How? Why? Similarly, consider the story of Balaam and his talking donkey in the book of Numbers,[1] which the Bible critics assign to E, a story so unified that even the Bible critics do not dare divide it. But they *should have* because the story of Balaam is constantly zigzagging between Hashem and Elokim.

Two Accounts of Creation?

Recall that the documentary hypothesis posits that P wrote the first account of creation in Genesis 1 and that P uses the name Elokim. It also states that J wrote the second account of creation and that J uses the name Hashem.

This is a half-truth. The second account does not only use Hashem, but rather a compound name, Hashem-Elokim. The two are compounded twenty times to be exact. In fact, the so-called second account of creation actually uses Elokim *more often* than it does Hashem, the name that is J's claim to fame. To get a sense of this, simply scan the bolded names of God in Genesis 1 below, a text that according to the Bible critics was authored by P.

Genesis 1: Creation

In the beginning **ELOKIM** created the heavens and the earth. The earth was astonishingly empty, with darkness upon the surface of the deep, and the *Ru'ach* **ELOKIM** (Divine Presence) hovered upon the surface of the waters. **ELOKIM** said: "Let there be light," and there was light. **ELOKIM** saw that the light was good, and **ELOKIM** separated between the light and the darkness. **ELOKIM** called to the light—"Day," and to the darkness He called— "Night." And there was evening and there was morning, one day. **ELOKIM** said: "Let there be a firmament in the midst of the waters, and let it separate between water and water." So **ELOKIM** made the firmament, and separated between the waters which were beneath the firmament and the waters which were above the firmament. And it was so. **ELOKIM** called to the firmament—"Heaven." And there was evening and there was morning, a second day. **ELOKIM** said: "Let the waters beneath the heaven be gathered into one area, and let the dry land appear." And it was so. **ELOKIM** called to the dry land—"Earth," and to the gathering of waters He called—"Seas." And **ELOKIM** saw that it was good. **ELOKIM** said: "Let the earth sprout vegetation—herbage yielding seed, fruit trees yielding fruit each after its kind, containing its own seed on the earth." And it was so. And the earth brought forth vegetation—herbage yielding seed after its kind, and trees yielding fruit, each containing its seed after its kind. And **ELOKIM** saw that it was good. And there was evening and there was morning, a third day. **ELOKIM** said: "Let there be luminaries in the firmament of the heaven to separate between the day and the night; and they shall serve as signs, and for festivals, and for days and years. And they shall serve as luminaries in the firmament of the heaven to shine upon the earth." And it was so. And **ELOKIM** made the two great luminaries, the greater luminary to dominate the day and the lesser luminary to dominate the night; and the stars. And **ELOKIM** set them in the firmament of the heaven to give light upon the earth, and to dominate by day and by night, and to separate between the light and the darkness. And **ELOKIM** saw that it was good. And there was evening and there was morning, a fourth day. **ELOKIM** said: "Let the waters teem with teeming living creatures, and fowl that fly about over the earth across the expanse of the heavens." And **ELOKIM** created the great sea-giants and every living being that creeps, with which the waters teemed after their kinds; and all winged fowl of every kind. And **ELOKIM** saw that it was good. **ELOKIM** blessed them, saying, "Be fruitful and multiply, and fill the waters in the seas; but the fowl shall increase on the earth." And there was evening and there was morning, a fifth day. **ELOKIM** said: "Let the earth bring forth living creatures, each according to its kind—animal, and creeping thing, and beast of the land each according to its kind." And it was so. **ELOKIM** made the beast of the earth according to its kind, and the animal according to its kind, and every creeping being of the ground according to its kind. And **ELOKIM** saw that it was good. And **ELOKIM** said: "Let us make Man in Our image, after Our likeness. They shall rule over the fish of the sea, the birds of the sky, and over the animal, the whole earth, and every creeping thing that creeps upon the earth." So **ELOKIM** created Man in His image, in the image of **ELOKIM** He created him; male and female He created them. **ELOKIM** blessed them and **ELOKIM** said to them, "Be fruitful and multiply, fill the earth and subdue it; and rule over the fish of the sea, the bird of the sky, and every living thing that moves on the earth." **ELOKIM** said: "Behold, I have given to you all herbage yielding seed that is on the surface of the entire earth, and every tree that has seed-yielding fruit; it shall be yours for food. And to every beast of the earth, to every bird of the sky, and to everything that moves on the earth, within which there is a living soul, every green herb is for food." And it was so. And **ELOKIM** saw all that He had made, and behold it was very good. And there was evening and there was morning, the sixth day.

Genesis 2: Sabbath

Thus the heaven and the earth were finished, and all their array. By the seventh day **ELOKIM** completed His work, which He had done, and He abstained on the seventh day from all His work, which He had done. **ELOKIM** blessed the seventh day and sanctified it because on it He abstained from all His work which **ELOKIM** created to make.

Now scan the bolded names of God in this text, which according to the Bible critics was authored by J.

Genesis 2–3: Garden of Eden

These are the chronicles of heaven and earth when they were created, on the day that **HASHEM ELOKIM** made earth and heaven. No shrub of the field was yet on earth nor had any grass of the field yet sprouted, because **HASHEM ELOKIM** had not brought rain upon the earth, and there was no man to work the ground. Then a mist rose up from the earth and watered the entire surface of the ground. **HASHEM ELOKIM** then formed man out of dust of the ground, and He breathed into his nostrils a soul of life, and man became a living being. **HASHEM ELOKIM** planted a garden to the east of Eden, and there He placed the man whom He had formed. **HASHEM ELOKIM** caused the ground to give forth every tree that is of pleasing appearance and good for food, as well as the Tree of Life in the middle of the garden, and the Tree of Knowledge of Good and Bad. A river flowed out of Eden to water the garden, and from there it divided and became four major rivers. The name of the first is Pishon; it is the one that encircles the entire land of Havilah, where gold is found. The gold of that land is good. Also found there are crystal and the

shoham stone. The name of the second river is Gihon; it is
the one that encircles the entire land of Cush. The name
of the third river is Hiddekel [i.e., Tigris], which flows to
the east of Assyria; and the fourth river is the Euphrates.
HASHEM ELOKIM took the man and placed him in
the Garden of Eden to cultivate it and guard it. **HASHEM
ELOKIM** commanded the man, saying, "Of every tree of
the garden you may freely eat; but of the Tree of Knowledge of Good and Bad you shall not eat, for on the day
you eat of it, you will surely die." **HASHEM ELOKIM**
said, "It is not good for man to be alone; I will make a
compatible helper for him." **HASHEM ELOKIM** had
formed out of the ground every wild beast and every bird
of heaven. He [now] brought them to the man to see what
he would name each one, and whatever the man called
each living thing remained its name. The man gave names
to every livestock animal and bird of the sky, as well as all
the wild beasts. But the man did not find a helper who was
compatible for himself. So **HASHEM ELOKIM** cast a
deep sleep upon the man, and he slept. He then took one
of his sides and closed the flesh in its place. **HASHEM
ELOKIM** built up the side that He had taken from the
man into a woman, and He brought her to the man. The
man said, "Now this is bone from my bones and flesh from
my flesh. She shall be called Woman, because she was taken
from man." A man shall therefore leave his father and his
mother and cleave to his wife, and they shall become one
flesh. The two of them were naked, the man and his wife,
but they felt no shame. Now the serpent was the most cunning of all the wild beasts that **HASHEM ELOKIM** had
made. He said to the woman, "Did **ELOKIM** really say,
'You may not eat from any of the trees of the garden?'"

Chapter 3

The woman replied to the serpent, "We may eat from the fruit of the trees of the garden. But as to the fruit of the tree that is in the middle of the garden, **ELO-KIM** said, 'You shall not eat of it, nor shall you touch it, lest you die.'" The serpent said to the woman, "You will certainly not die! For **ELOKIM** knows that on the day you eat from it your eyes will be opened, and you will be like **ELOKIM**, knowing good and evil." The woman saw that the tree was good for eating and desirable to the eyes, and that the tree was attractive as a means to gain intelligence. So she took some of its fruit and ate, and also gave some to her husband with her, and he ate. Then the eyes of both of them were opened, and they realized that they were naked. They sewed together fig leaves, and made themselves loincloths. They heard the voice of **HASHEM ELOKIM** who was moving about in the garden in the direction of day's end, so the man and his wife hid themselves from **HASHEM ELOKIM** among the trees of the garden. **HASHEM ELOKIM** called to the man and said to him, "Where are you?" He replied, "I heard Your voice in the garden, and I was afraid because I am naked, so I hid." So He said, "Who told you that you are naked? Did you eat of the tree from which I commanded you not to eat?" The man replied, "The woman whom You gave to be with me—she gave me of the tree, and I ate." **HASHEM ELOKIM** then said to the woman, "What is this that you have done?" The woman replied, "The serpent deceived me, and I ate." Then **HASHEM ELOKIM** said to the serpent, "Because you did this, accursed are you more than all the livestock and all the wild beasts. On your belly you shall move, and dust you shall eat, all the days of your life. I will plant hatred between you and the woman, and between your offspring and her offspring. He will strike you in the head, and you will strike him in the heel." To the woman He said, "I will greatly increase your anguish and [the distress of] your pregnancy. In anguish will you give birth to children. Your longing will be for your husband, and he will dominate you." And to the man He said, "Because you listened to your wife, and ate of the tree about which I commanded you, saying, 'Do not eat from it,' the earth will be cursed for you. With anguish will you derive food from it all the days of your life. Thorns and thistles will it bring forth for you, and you will eat the grass of the field. By the sweat of your brow shall you eat bread—until you return to the ground, for from it you were taken. For you are dust, and to dust you shall return." The man named his wife Eve, because she was the mother of all the living. And **HASHEM ELOKIM** made leather garments for the man and his wife and He clothed them. **HASHEM ELOKIM** said, "Behold, now that the man has become like the Unique One among us, knowing good and evil, what if he should stretch forth his hand and also take from the Tree of Life and eat, and live forever!" **HASHEM ELOKIM** thereupon banished him from the Garden of Eden, to work the ground from which he was taken. He drove the man out, and at the east of the Garden of Eden He stationed the Cherubim and the revolving sword blade, to guard the path to the Tree of Life.

A simple reading of the foregoing text attests to three undisputed facts:

1. In Genesis 2-3, God is almost always referred to as Hashem-Elokim;

2. This compound name appears in this story alone. In no other story in the Bible is God referred to consistently as Hashem-Elokim.[2]

3. God is referred to as just Elokim four times, all in the conversation in which the snake tempts Eve to sin.

These three facts are easily explained. First, why does the author use the unusual compound "Hashem-Elokim" in chapters 2 and 3 *and only* in chapters 2 and 3?

It seems that the Bible's author understood that readers might one day notice that the Creation story uses Elokim, while the Garden of Eden story uses Hashem, and conclude: "The different names must represent two different gods, or two different authors writing about God from different perspectives."

Therefore the author wisely used the compound term Hashem-Elokim in order to point out that Hashem in the story of the Garden of Eden is the very same Elokim of Creation. Once this point was made clear by the repetition of Hashem-Elokim well over a dozen times, it no longer needed repeating.

Why does the passage involving the snake drop the name Hashem? Could it be because the author did not want to associate God's personal and holy name with talk of sin or dialogue with a lowly snake?

Exceptions to the Rule

The Bible critics' hypothetical rules about the names of God are breached time and again, even in the book of Genesis, with its supposedly clear boundaries between J, E, and P. Here are examples of J using "E-L" or "ELOKIM" (P's and E's names for God) and of P and E using "HASHEM" (J's name for God).

EXCEPTIONS IN THE BOOK OF GENESIS

E USES HASHEM	P USES "HASHEM"	J USES "ELOKIM"
"Then Jacob took a vow, saying: 'If ELOKIM will be with me, will guard me on this way that I am going; will give me bread to eat and clothes to wear, and I return in peace to my father's house, and HASHEM will be an ELOKIM to me, then this stone which I have set up as a pillar shall become a house of ELOKIM, and whatever You will give me, I shall repeatedly tithe to You.'" (Genesis 28:20–22)	"And HASHEM did for Sarah as He had spoken." (Genesis 21:1) "HASHEM appeared to Abram and said to him . . ." (Genesis 17:1)	"Now when man began to increase on the face of the earth and daughters were born to them, the sons of ELOKIM saw that the daughters of man were fair, and they took them-selves wives from whomever they chose. And HASHEM said: 'My spirit will no longer dwell in man for long periods of time; inasmuch as he too is flesh. So let his term in the future be shortened to only a hundred and twenty years.' "The giants were on the earth in those days and also later, when the sons of ELOKIM consorted with the daughters of man and they bore them children. They were the mighty ones of old, men of renown." (Genesis 6:1–4)
		"And he (Noah) said: 'Blessed is HASHEM, the God of Shem . . . May ELOKIM extend Japheth, but He will dwell in the tents of Shem . . .'" (Genesis 9:26–27)
		"He (Isaac) said: 'See, the fragrance of my son is like the fragrance of a field which HASHEM had blessed—And may ELOKIM give you of the dew of the heavens . . .'" (Genesis 27:27–28)
		". . . How can then I perpetrate this great evil and have sinned against ELOKIM!" (Genesis 39:9)
		"Joseph said to them on the third day: 'Do this and live; I fear ELOKIM. . . .'" (Genesis 42:18)
		". . . Their hearts sank, and they turned trembling one to another, saying: 'What is this that ELOKIM has done to us?'" (Genesis 42:28)
		"Then he (Joseph) lifted up his eyes and saw his brother Benjamin, his mother's son, so he said: '. . . ELOKIM be gracious to you, my son.'" (Genesis 43:29)
		"So Judah said: 'What can we say to my lord? How can we speak? And how can we justify ourselves? ELOKIM has un-covered the sin of your servants. . . .'" (Genesis 44:16)
		"And now, be not distressed, nor reproach yourself for having sold me here, for it was to be a provider that ELOKIM sent me ahead of you. . . . Thus ELOKIM has sent me ahead of you to ensure your survival . . . It was not you who sent me here, but ELOKIM . . . Hurry—go up to my father and say to him: 'So said your son Joseph: ELOKIM has made me a master of all Egypt . . .'" (Genesis 45:5–9)
		"[That was] from the E-L (GOD) of your father and He will help you, and with SHA-DAI—and He will bless you [with] blessings of heaven from above, blessings of the deep crouching below, blessings of the bosom and womb." (Genesis 49:25)—(J or Other [no consensus among critics])

"Repairing" Some Exceptions—by Splitting Verses

In regard to the examples above, the Bible critics generally admit that J, E, and P violate their rules and use each other's names for God. But on other occasions the Bible critics lose patience with their own sources' deviant behavior because "too many" exceptions strain their rules. So the Bible critics come up with another tactic. In order to force the sources to behave, they steal parts of a verse written by one source and give it to another, as in the three examples below.[3]

KEY: J *E* P D̲ R̠

They that came [into the ark]—came male and female . . .
as ELOKIM had commanded him;
And HASHEM encompassed him.
Genesis 7:16, P & **J**

She [Rachel] conceived and bore a son, and said: "ELOKIM has taken away my disgrace."
So she called his name Joseph, saying:
"May HASHEM add on for me another son."
Genesis 30:23-24, *E,* R̠, & **J**

And HASHEM saw that he (Moses) turned to see.
And ELOKIM called to him from inside the bush . . .
Exodus 3:4, **J** & *E*

• • •

The Bible critics were aware of these problems, and they came up with an answer that is refuted in its entirety in Appendix

A. In short, the Bible critics claim that starting from Exodus 3, E begins using the name Hashem, and starting from Exodus 6, P, too, begins using the name Hashem.

Exodus, of course, is only the second of the Five Books of Moses. In other words, the critics themselves say their claim that different names equal different authors holds up for only one book and a little of the next. Yes—*their entire hypothesis is based on no more than a fifth of the Five Books of Moses.* And as we've already shown, even that one-fifth (the book of Genesis) is riddled with exceptions: E uses Hashem, P uses Hashem, and J uses Elokim.

Deconstructing the Names of God Once and for All

The Bible critics' explanation of the names of God obscures a very simple fact that has been known for years in academic circles and for millennia in Jewish tradition: Elokim and Hashem are not competing names for the Deity at all, but they are names that mean two different things. Hashem is a proper noun (as in George Washington) and Elokim is a common noun (as in president). In other words, Hashem is God's personal name and his title is Elokim, which translates best as God (stemming from the word E-L, meaning "strength" in Hebrew and ancient Canaanite. Elokim, which has a plural form, implies "The One Who Holds All the Powers" or "All Powerful" or "Almighty." This term for God reflects the Jewish concept of monotheism).

As an example of this distinction, let us examine a well-known verse, which, ironically, happens to be an instance of J crossing the line and using the name Elokim. In Genesis 9, when Noah blesses Shem (Abraham's ancestor), he uses Hashem; when he blesses his other son Japheth, he uses Elokim:

"And he said, 'Blessed is HASHEM, the God of Shem; and let Canaan be a slave to them. May ELOKIM extend Japheth, but he

will dwell in the tents of Shem; may Canaan be a slave to them.'"
(Genesis 9:26–27)

The reason for the switch is crystal clear. Shem, the forefather of Abraham, is blessed with the name Hashem, which will be used by his descendants, the Israelites. Japheth, on the other hand, is blessed with the name Elokim, having a connection to God, but not the Jewish concept of God (i.e., a God who is concerned with the actions of man, who rewards and punishes, and who is the ultimate source of morality). Interestingly, the book of Genesis tells us that Japheth was the forefather of the Greeks, who gave us "the god of the philosophers"—Aristotle's perfectly complete but utterly distant and indifferent "first mover," the god with no name.

Jean Astruc, the eighteenth-century French amateur Bible critic, did not understand this distinction and misread the opening chapters of Genesis as two different stories. Generations of scholars have worked heroically trying to keep the hypothesis alive, but in so doing have cut off the body (Exodus through Deuteronomy) and have performed unnecessary operations on the decapitated head (Genesis).

There never was any need for such emergency procedures. The Bible has always been a complete whole when read without ideological blinders. What the Bible critics call the "first account of creation," but what we refer to as simply the Creation story (Genesis 1), is about the universal God creating heaven and earth. And what they call the "second account of creation," but what we refer to as the Garden of Eden story (Genesis 2–3), introduces the name Hashem, reflecting an intimate relationship between man and God. In this story, God commands, rewards, admonishes, and punishes. But as explained above, in order not to confuse the reader into mistaking these two names for two different gods, the Garden of Eden story uses the compound name Hashem-Elokim.

With this simple theory we can explain almost every single shift in the uses of Hashem and Elokim in Genesis.[4] But this has been done before and needs no repetition.[5]

The first and strongest proof of the documentary hypothesis, the Names of God argument, was based on the mistaken view that Hashem and Elokim were synonyms for God. This was never true. Had the Bible critics known this, the documentary hypothesis never would have gotten off the ground.

PART II

Academic Malpractice

CHAPTER SIX

Believing Is Seeing

The critics find confirmation for preconceived notions

Bible critics describe their procedure for investigating Bible texts as the "critical method" or the "historical–critical method." However they define it, its results compare unfavorably with the more familiar "scientific method" that we all had to learn in grade school and that scientists have successfully used to collect data, to test hypotheses, and to make predictions. We can distill the essence of the Bible critics' method as follows:

1. Create a position first, then use any evidence to support it.
2. When the evidence does not support one's position, tamper with the evidence.

We will look at the first step in this chapter and the second in the next.

There Is Madness to Their Method

Imagine a group of music professors analyzing Beethoven's Fifth Symphony. They observe that the great musical composition uses both a clarinet and a cello in some of the same movements. This arouses their suspicion. The instruments have a similar range, and it seems a dubious practice to use them both at the same time.

Then they notice that the clarinet consistently plays high notes and the cello plays low notes. They run to their department chair with their discovery that Beethoven's Fifth is really two compositions that were somehow blended together.

As the professors develop their thesis, they note that clarinet and cello both begin with the same letter, C. They astutely choose the letters H for "high" (clarinet) and L for "low" (cello), satisfied that the cello sounds a little like both "L" and "low."

The more they explore their theory, the more convincing it is to them. That is because the clarinet is far more likely to use an E-flat, whereas the cello lines tend to revolve around a B-flat.

Of course it is not so simple as all that. Nuances abound. Knowledge of H and L expands geometrically through prodigious amounts of circular reasoning. All it takes is an initial identification of the musical instrument, and the musicologists can tell you whether H or L wrote it; if a B-flat motif arises they know that it came from the original L source, even if the musical redactor now has the cello playing a high part. But that's what the professionals are paid for, sorting out these compositional complexities.

This is the Bible's critical method at work.

For example, after explaining that J uses Hashem (YHWH) and E uses Elokim (also E-L), Richard Elliott Friedman writes: "For the entire Torah, the picture is as follows: The names YHWH and E-L and the word God (Elokim) occur more than two thousand times, and the number of exceptions to this picture is three. Despite this phenomenal fact, we still find writers on this subject asserting that 'the names of God' do not prove anything."[1]

The Bible critics divide up the Torah based on the names of God. The use of Hashem (in Genesis) for them signals J's authorship, and Elokim signals E's and P's. Then the Bible critics have the chutzpah to claim that the fact that Hashem always appears in J (whose existence they first posited based on his use of Hashem) and that Elokim is used in E and P (whom they also posited precisely on the grounds that both use Elokim) somehow proves their theory.

Logically, their own division of the sources cannot be used as evidence of the theory. That is like firing the arrow and then drawing the target around it after it lands.

A prominent example of this kind of reasoning is how the Bible critics decided to take all the priestly laws and dump them on P. After all, the sensitive artiste who wrote the beautiful stories of the Garden of Eden (J) could not have been interested in all the prosaic details and ritual involved in the construction of the Tabernacle. Once again, Friedman gives voice to this line of thinking:

"Ages, dates, measurements, numbers, orders, and precise instructions are an obvious, major concern in P. There is nothing even nearly comparable in degree in J, E, or D."[2]

But, of course, this will happen when all issues in the Bible that deal with "ages, dates, measurements, numbers, orders, and precise instructions" are given to P. It would work just as well if we began with the premise that all the cello sections in Beethoven's Fifth were written by L and the clarinet sections by H. Then well we might say that whenever the clarinet spoke, "there is nothing even comparable in degree in L."

Showdown between Moses and Pharaoh

Intelligent readers may find it hard to believe that sophisticated and highly trained scholars could seriously follow such a method. But they do. Consider the story of the Ten Plagues—one of the most memorable episodes in the Bible. Its searing political demand, "Let My people go . . ." has been an inspiration to freedom seekers through the ages. Given its dramatic power and monumental status in the collective consciousness of our civilization, readers may be surprised to learn that the Bible critics believe the story of the Ten

Plagues was cobbled together from E and P. Before we examine the Bible critics' claims for dual authorship, let's remind ourselves of the story.

God has decided that it is time to redeem Egypt's Hebrew slaves, and He recruits a reluctant Moses to confront Pharaoh, granting Moses the assistance of his brother Aaron. God says: "See, I have made you a master over Pharaoh, and Aaron your brother shall be your spokesman." (Exodus 7:1)

God, in effect, is setting up a duel between Moses and Pharaoh, with Moses' brother Aaron and Pharaoh's necromancers acting as "seconds," and each of their staffs as the weapon of choice.

> Hashem said to Moses and Aaron, saying: "When Pharaoh speaks to you, saying, 'Provide a wonder for yourselves,' you shall say to Aaron, "Take your staff and cast it down before Pharaoh—it will become a crocodile!" Moses came with Aaron to Pharaoh and they did so, as Hashem had commanded; Aaron cast down his staff before Pharaoh and before his servants, and it became a crocodile. Pharaoh, too, summoned his wise men and sorcerers, and they, too—the necromancers of Egypt—did so with their incantations. Each one cast down his staff and they became crocodiles; and the staff of Aaron swallowed their staffs. (Exodus 7:8–12)

The duel resumes at the Nile, scene of the first plague, in Exodus 7:14–20. Once again, Moses takes on Pharaoh, and Aaron the necromancers. Moses uses his staff to turn the Nile into blood. In the vast pantheon of Egyptian gods, the Nile was a chief god associated with Pharaoh; hence Moses was essentially facing off with Pharaoh. Aaron, on the other hand, uses his staff to turn all the other waters of Egypt into blood.

So the river was full of blood because of Moses, and there was blood throughout the rest of Egypt because of Aaron. Once again the necromancers do "the same" as Aaron. They're still competing with him. (Exodus 7:21–22)

Pharaoh remains unimpressed since his magicians can do the same as Aaron, whom he undoubtedly regards as Moses' magician. Pharaoh never even asks Moses to stop the plague—it just ends after seven days, during which time the Egyptians were able to dig for sources of drinkable water. (Exodus 7:23–25)

The contest continues in the second plague. Moses tells his "number two" to perform his magic. Aaron stretches out his hand with his staff and soon frogs cover the land of Egypt. Immediately thereafter, the necromancers match Aaron's magic with their own. This plague evidently bothered Pharaoh more than the previous one because he asks Moses to entreat God to stop it. (Exodus 7:26–8:11)

In the third plague as well, Moses' magician, Aaron, stretches out his staff—his magic wand, as it were—and strikes the dust of the land, which then turns into lice throughout the land of Egypt. (Exodus 8:12–15)

What is different about the above verses is that this time Pharaoh's magicians cannot replicate the magic. They admit this level of sorcery is out of their league. ("It is a finger of God!") Moses' second had bested Pharaoh's second. From here on the rest of the story is just Moses versus Pharaoh.[3]

If you have followed our story so far, you undoubtedly perceive a beautifully framed, coherent narrative. The Bible critics disagree. They divide the story between P and E.

They divide it based not on any ancient Bible fragments or even modern, sophisticated computer analyses. Operating at a comic-book level of literary analysis, they circle the words "Aaron" and "necromancers" in crayon and give all those passages to P on the theory that P was a big fan of Aaron and was also into magic. The rest of the text they attribute to E, supposedly a big fan of Moses. All the care the Bible's author took to develop this story flies out the window.

This is the "critical method" laid bare. The Bible critics are so busy making tiny circles that they fail to see the big picture.[4]

The Bible Critics Divide P from E in the Ten Plagues Story

(Exodus 7:8–8:15)

KEY: P *E*

Introduction

(P) Hashem said to Moses and Aaron, saying: "When Pharaoh speaks to you, saying: 'Provide a wonder for yourselves,' you shall say to Aaron: "Take your staff and cast it down before Pharaoh—it will become a crocodile!" Moses came with Aaron to Pharaoh and they did so, as Hashem had commanded; Aaron cast down his staff before Pharaoh and before his servants, and it became a crocodile. Pharaoh, too, summoned his wise men and sorcerers, and they, too—the necromancers of Egypt—did so with their incantations. Each one cast down his staff and they became crocodiles; and the staff of Aaron swallowed their staffs. The heart of Pharaoh was strong and he did not heed them, as Hashem had spoken.

First Plague: Blood

(E) Hashem said to Moses: "Pharaoh's heart is stubborn, he refuses to send the people. Go to Pharaoh in the morning—behold! He goes out to the water—and you shall stand opposite him at the River's bank, and the staff that was turned into a snake you shall

take in your hand." You shall say to him: "Hashem, the God of the Hebrews, has sent me to you, saying—'Send out My people that they may serve Me in the Wilderness—but behold, you have not heeded up to now.'" So says Hashem: "Through this shall you know that I am Hashem; behold, with the staff that is in my hand I shall strike the waters that are in the River, and they shall change to blood. The fish-life that is in the water shall die and the River shall become foul. Egypt will grow weary of trying to drink water from the River." (P) Hashem said to Moses: "Say to Aaron: 'Take your staff and stretch out your hand over the waters of Egypt—over their rivers, over their canals, over their reservoirs, and over all their gatherings of water, and they shall become blood; there shall be blood throughout the land of Egypt, even in the wooden and stone vessels.'" Moses and Aaron did so, as Hashem had commanded. *(E) He held the staff aloft and struck the water that was in the River in the presence of Pharaoh and in the presence of his servants, and all the water that was in the River changed to blood. The fish-life that was in the River died and the River became foul; Egypt could not drink water from the River, and the blood was throughout the land of Egypt.* (P) The necromancers of Egypt did the same by means of their incantations; so Pharaoh's heart was strong and he did not heed them, as Hashem had spoken. *(E) Pharaoh turned away and came to his palace. He did not take this to heart either. All of the Egyptians dug roundabout the River for water to drink, for they could not drink from the waters of the River. Seven days were completed after Hashem struck the River.*

Second Plague: Frogs

(E) Hashem said to Moses: "Come to Pharaoh and say to him, 'So said Hashem—Send out My people that they may serve Me.

But if you refuse to send out, behold, I shall strike your entire boundary with frogs. The River shall swarm with frogs, and they shall ascend and come into your palace and your bedroom and your bed, and into the house of your servants and of your people, and into your ovens and into your kneading bowls. And into you and your people and all your servants will the frogs ascend."' (P) Hashem said to Moses: "Say to Aaron: 'Stretch out your hand with your staff over the rivers, over the canals, and over the reservoirs, and raise up the frogs over the land of Egypt.'"

Aaron stretched out his hand over the waters of Egypt, and the frog-infestation ascended and covered the land of Egypt. The necromancers did the same through their incantations, *(E) and they brought up the frogs upon the land of Egypt. Pharaoh summoned Moses and Aaron and said: "Entreat Hashem that He remove the frogs from me and my people, and I shall send out the people that they may bring offerings to Hashem." Moses said to Pharaoh: "Glorify yourself over me—for when should I entreat for you, for your servants, and for your people, to excise the frogs from you and from your houses? Only in the River shall they remain." And he said: "For tomorrow." He said: "As you say, so that you will know that there is none like Hashem, our God. The frogs will depart from you and your houses, and from your servants and your people; only in the River shall they remain." Moses and Aaron left Pharaoh's presence; Moses cried out to Hashem concerning the frogs that he had inflicted upon Pharaoh. Hashem carried out the word of Moses, and the frogs died—from the houses, from the courtyards, and from the fields. They piled them up into heaps and heaps, and the land stank. Pharaoh saw that there had been a relief, and kept making his heart stubborn. He did not heed them, as Hashem had spoken.*

Third Plague: Lice

(P) Hashem said to Moses: "Say to Aaron: 'Stretch out your staff and strike the dust of the land; it shall become lice throughout the land of Egypt.'" So they did; Aaron stretched out his hand with his staff and struck the dust of the land, and the lice-infestation was on man and beast; all the dust of the land became lice, throughout the land of Egypt. The sorcerers did the same with their incantations to draw forth the lice, but they could not. And the lice-infestation was on man and beast. The sorcerers said to Pharaoh: "It is a finger of God!" But Pharaoh's heart was strong and he did not heed them, as Hashem had spoken.

CHAPTER SEVEN

Tampering with the Evidence

The critics establish rules, break them,
then cover up their crime

The core of the Bible critics' method is to use their own assumptions to prove . . . their own assumptions. They determine that P is biased toward Aaron and E toward Moses, then carve up the Ten Plagues story depending upon who is getting center stage at the moment. They endow P with ages, dates, measurements, and priestly legislation, and then take those same criteria to establish P's authorship.

This circularity, however, creates unforeseen problems for the Bible critics. They now have rigid personalities in J, E, P, and D, who don't always play their roles so neatly. Thus the critics have resorted to a second step in their critical method to deal with situations in which the evidence does not support their preconceptions: they tamper with the evidence.

For example, the genealogical histories in the book of Genesis—all of the "begats" in the biblical family trees—usually begin with the Hebrew words *eyleh toldot*, which means "these are the generations of . . ." or "this is the history of . . ."

The problem for the documentary hypothesis is that these oft-recurring genealogies often appear in the middle of passages assigned to J (who uses Hashem), or P (who uses Elokim). Their solution? R did it.

The chart below shows instances of *eyleh toldot*, the sources to whom the Bible critics assign credit (usually R), and the sources that *should* have been credited if the Bible critics' faith in their alphabet of authors were strong enough to obviate the invention of R.[1]

"THIS IS THE HISTORY OF . . ."		
Source in Genesis	The Bible critics assign it to:	According to the Bible critics' logic, the author should be:
"This is the history of the heaven and earth . . ." (2:4a & 2:4b)	R (2:4a) & J (2:4b)	J
"This is the book of the history of Man . . ." (5:1)[2]	P or Other	P or Other
"This is the history of Noah . . ." (6:9)	R	P
"And this is the history of the sons of Noah . . ." (10:1)	R	P
"This is the history of Shem . . ." (11:10)	R	P or Other
"And this is the history of Terach . . ." (11:27)	R	P
"And this is the history of Ishmael . . ." (25:12)	R	P
"And this is the history of Isaac . . ." (25:19)	R	P
"And this is the history of Esau . . ." (36:1)	R	P
"This is the history of Jacob . . ." (37:2)	R	J

"This is the history of . . ." is a unique phrase, yet it occurs in both J and P texts. This is a problem, so they call out R. Having R on hand is like keeping a well-stocked bar in a room full of recovering alcoholics. Even the most circumspect scholar might yield to the temptation of using him to get through the dark moments.

Let's look at the Bible's very first "This is the history of . . ." (*eyleh toldot*) starting at Genesis 2:4.[3]

> This is the history of the heavens and the earth when they were created, in the day that Hashem Elokim made earth and heaven. Now no thorns of the field were yet in the earth, and no grain of the field had yet sprouted, for Hashem Elokim had not caused it to rain upon the earth, and there was no man to work the ground, but the waters of the deep went up from the earth and watered the whole face of the ground. Then Hashem Elokim formed the man of dust from the ground, and breathed into his nostrils the soul of life; and man became a living being.

We cannot progress through even a single complete sentence before the Bible critics hack into this elegant prose. That is because the latest fashion in Bible criticism is to divide the introductory verse into two as follows:[4]

> 2:4a This is the history of the heavens and the earth when they were created. (P)
>
> 2:4b **in the day that Hashem Elokim made earth and heaven. (J)**

So 2:4a is claimed to be the conclusion of the first account of creation (Genesis 1) and therefore written by P. Meanwhile, 2:4b, though only a fragment of a sentence, is seen as the introduction to the second account of creation (Genesis 2 and 3) written by J.

What impels the Bible critics to reach for the scalpel? Remember, they cut up the Bible based on certain preconceived notions.

The Bible critics simply assume ancient writers are incapable of or uninterested in varying their diction. Therefore, the Bible critics claim that P uniquely uses the word "created" (*bara*), whereas J uses the word "made" or "formed" (*asot* or *yatzar*).

Indeed, throughout the story of Creation in Genesis 1 we find the word "created." But in the Garden of Eden story in Genesis 2–3 we find "made" or "formed." Within these first three chapters of Genesis there is only one problem. In verse 2:4, where the Garden of Eden narrative begins, both words are used.

So J is using an unauthorized word that only P uses ("created"). How are the Bible critics going to deal with a contradiction in their hypothesis?

You can judge people's character by how they act in demanding situations, when they are being tested. The Bible critics flunk this test by tampering with the evidence. Their overarching commitment to the notion that J didn't know or wouldn't consider using the word "created" (or that only J would use the name Hashem) leads to the massacre of a beautiful verse.

IF THE CRITICS DIDN'T TAMPER . . .	
Genesis 1:1 assigned to P	**Genesis 2:4 should be assigned to J**
"In the Beginning ELOKIM created the heavens and the earth. . . . "	
	"This is the history of the heavens and the earth when they were created."
	"In the day that Hashem Elokim made earth and heaven."

. . . BUT THEY DO!	
Genesis 1:1 & 2:4a assigned to P	**Genesis 2:4b Stays J**
"In the Beginning ELOKIM created the heavens and the earth. . . ."	
". . .This is the history of the heavens and the earth when they were created."	
	"In the day that Hashem Elokim made earth and heaven."

And yet after all this fuss, the consensus of Bible critics credit the word "created" to J later on in Genesis 6:7. In fact, the same verse also contains the word "made," just as in Genesis 2:4. Why don't the Bible critics insist on breaking up that verse as well?

J *DOES* VARY HIS DICTION

"And Hashem said, 'I will blot out man whom I CREATED from the face of the ground—from man to animal, to creeping things, and to birds of the sky; for I have reconsidered my having MADE them.'" (Genesis 6:7)

So the Bible critics place their scholarly credentials on the line to cover up for J; they tamper with the evidence to protect their guy's image. And then J lets his supporters twist in the wind, breaking the law by using "created." Adding insult to injury, he uses "made" in the same sentence.

As redacted by the Bible critics, the Creation narrative ends with a summary statement from Genesis 2:4a: "This is the history of the heavens and the earth when they were created." But this is a grave error. The phrase, "This is the history of . . ." (*eyleh toldot*), always points ahead to what comes after, never to the subject matter that precedes it. This is true in every instance in the Bible. Take a look at Genesis 5:1 and Numbers 3:1, each shown with the preceding verse (which clearly concludes a section), and the following verse (which clearly forms part of the new section):

From the book of Genesis:

4:26 And as for Seth, to him also a son was born, and he named him Enosh. Then to call in the Name of Hashem became profaned.

5:1 This is the history of the descendants of Adam—on the day that Elokim created Man, He made him in the likeness of Elokim.

5:2 He created them male and female. He blessed them and called their name Man on the day they were created.

From the book of Numbers:

2:34 The Children of Israel did everything that Hashem had commanded Moses—so they encamped according to their banners and so they journeyed; every man according to his families, by his father's household.

3:1 This is the history of Aaron and Moses on the day Hashem spoke with Moses at Mount Sinai.

3:2 These are the names of the sons of Aaron, the firstborn was Nadab, and Abihu, Elazar, and Itamar.

These are but two examples of the exceptionless formula whereby the words "This is the history of . . ." clearly describe only what comes afterward. Yet, the Bible critics break the rule by using Genesis 2:4a to describe what comes before.

To the crimes of evidence tampering and faulty scholarship must be added a third charge of violence against the literary integrity of Genesis 2:4. In sawing it in half, the Bible critics ignore the fact that this opening verse is a chiasmus, the Bible's dominant literary form, which we discuss later in the book. For now, however, simply note that the verse has a simple and beautiful symmetry:

1. This is the history of the heavens and the earth
    2. When they were created.

    2.' In the day that Hashem Elokim made
1.' Earth and heaven.

Just a little biblical poetry, that is all. Hence the redundancy and the change of word order ("heaven and earth" and later "earth and heaven").[5]

"Heavy" Handed Marshaling of Evidence: A Weak Case for the Use of "Strong"

The crime and cover-up involved in the Bible critics' treatment of Genesis 2:4 is not about a mistake of interpretation. It is about a flaw in their methodology and their unwillingness to treat the Bible on its own terms as a text that is read from beginning to end without preconceived notions. This methodology is on full display in the Bible critics' analysis of the story of the Ten Plagues, during which God famously hardens Pharaoh's heart. Specifically, the book of Exodus uses two words in describing Pharaoh's heart: "strong" and "heavy," which the critics assume to be synonyms pointing to two authors, P and E.

Rather than search for a reason for the author's varied diction, they instead try to score a point for their hypothesis based on the notion that two words imply two authors. They claim Pharaoh's heart is said to be "heavy" by E, who is credited with most of the Exodus narrative. Whenever Pharaoh's heart is described as "strong," that is allegedly a P text. The Bible critics' analysis, charted below, leaves the impression of a major linguistic cleavage between E and P.[6]

PHARAOH'S HEART		
VERSES IN EXODUS	**EXPRESSION**	**AUTHOR**
7:14; 8:11, 28; 9:7, 34; 10:1	*Pharaoh's heart: HEAVY*	E
7:13, 22; 8:15; 9:12; 14:4, 8, 17	Pharaoh's heart: STRONG	P

Looks impressive. But it is terribly misleading.

The passages attributed by the critics to P do use only "strong" in describing Pharaoh's heart. But that's not the same as saying that P alone uses that word. Exodus 4:21, a passage generally attributed to E, also says Pharaoh's heart was "strong." Then E uses it again in Exodus 9:35 in the plague of hail. And again in Exodus 10:20, Exodus 10:27, and in Exodus 11:10.

E uses this supposedly unique P idiom describing Pharaoh's heart as "strong" a nearly equal number of times as his own patented term "heavy" per the chart below:

PHARAOH'S HEART		
E	**EXPRESSION**	
Blood (7:14)	*HEAVY*	THE RULE: SIX TIMES
Frogs (8:11)	*HEAVY*	
Wild Beasts (8:28)	*HEAVY*	
Pestilence (9:7)	*HEAVY*	
Hail (9:34)	*HEAVY*	
Locust (10:1)	*HEAVY*	
Before the Plagues (4:21)	*STRONG*	EXCEPTIONS TO THE RULE: FIVE TIMES
Hail (9:35)	*STRONG*	
Locusts (10:20)	*STRONG*	
Darkness (10:27)	*STRONG*	
Firstborn (11:10)	*STRONG*	

That's like saying you are the undefeated winner when you break .500.

Foolishness of the "R"gument

The Bible critics can say that there were multiple documents that R fused together. But it is impossible to prove a negative, i.e., that R does not exist. The critics establish rules, break them, then use R to patch up the holes. In doing so, they make their hypothesis untestable and hence invalid.

In the three cases we hav e examined, the Bible critics were faced with choices.

We saw, for example, that the genealogical sections of Genesis, always beginning with the distinctive phrase, "This is the history of . . ." (*eyleh toldot*), recur throughout text that the Bible critics already assigned to J, E, or P. But these three authors can't all write their family histories in exactly the same way. So naturally they let R be the culprit.

J is supposed to use "made," not "created," but then is found to use both words in the same sentence. Rather than question their hypothesis, the Bible critics create an elaborate justification, dividing a verse in half, even though this creates further problems down the road (as when a supposed J verse again uses both those words).

When P is given "strong" and E "heavy," but E is found to use "strong" nearly as much as "heavy," the Bible critics justify their choice by dumping all the many redundancies into their "errors account," R.[7]

Just as evidence tampering by police (who control the supply of most or all of the evidence) is considered a major vulnerability of the trial system, so, too, must we be on guard against Bible critics who feel they alone have the special "training" to read a Bible verse and determine its origin.

Whether evidence tampering occurs because it is easier than performing the hard work of honest evidence collection or to justify or cover up a crime, it is an assault on truth and fairness. Indefensibly, the Bible critics have tampered with reason-based rules of evidence, misled Bible readers, and blinded themselves to the simple, elegant, and compelling case for the unity of the text.

CHAPTER EIGHT

Do Identical Twins Have a Common Parent?

"Multiple" authors possess surprising commonalities of style

As we have seen, the field of modern Bible criticism got its start when eighteenth-century European scholars observed that the book of Genesis used different names for God and appeared to be telling the story of Creation in two different ways. Since then scholars have focused on these fairly superficial differences while ignoring the most striking of similarities.

The Bible critics are like those who observe two identical twins and conclude that they are unrelated because they utter different words. E may be a narrator and P a legislator, but when E legislates he does it exactly the same way P does. If identical twins can be presumed to have a common parent, it is fair to conclude that the striking parallels among J, E, P, and D imply a common author.

As an example, let's look at the very beginning of the supposedly different accounts of creation found in Genesis 1 and Genesis 2–3.[1] Notice their identical structure:

First Account—Genesis 1:1–3 (P)

 (a) **Introduction**—"In the beginning Elokim created the heavens and the earth."

  (b) **Background**—"And the earth was astonishingly empty."

  (b) **Background**—"with darkness upon the surface of the deep."

   (c) **Preparation**—"and the Divine Presence hovered upon the surface of the waters."

    (d) **Creation**—"And Elokim said: 'Let there be light.'"

Second Account—Genesis 2:4–7 (J)

 (a) **Introduction**—"This is the history of the heavens and the earth when they were created, in the day that Hashem Elokim made earth and heaven."

  (b) **Background**—"Now no thorns of the field were yet on the earth."

  (b) **Background**—"and no grain of the field had yet sprouted. . . ."

   (c) **Preparation**—"But the waters of the deep went up from the earth and watered the whole surface of ground."

    (d) **Creation**—"And Hashem Elokim formed the man of dust from the ground."

Not only are these two stories of creation parallel in form, but they echo one another in substance as well. The two introductions are about the heavens and earth; the four background statements are all about voids; the two preparatory statements are about surfaces; and the two concluding statements both describe acts of creation.

The parallels in the "two accounts of creation" do not end

with the structure of these first few verses. The Bible's author leaves his mark through a variety of unique style elements. For example, chapter 1 of Genesis begins counting with a cardinal number and then switches to ordinals. Chapter 2 of Genesis does the same. For extra measure, we add an example from the book of Numbers. Notice that, according to the Bible critics, P wrote the first, J the second, and E the third:

FROM CARDINAL TO ORDINAL NUMBERS		
P	J	E
"And it was evening and it was morning, ONE day. . . . And it was evening and it was morning, a SECOND day. . . . And it was evening and it was morning, a THIRD day. . . ." (Genesis 1:5, 8, 13)	"A river issues forth from Eden to water the garden and from there it is divided and becomes four head-waters: The name of the ONE is Pishon. The name of the SECOND river is Gihon . . . The name of the THIRD river is Hiddekel . . ." (Genesis 2:10–14)	"Two men remained behind in the camp, the name of ONE was Eldad, And the name of the SECOND was Meidad . . ." (Numbers 11:26)

Moreover, God uses an unusual plural form of Self-description in Genesis 1 (P), and again in Genesis 3—and later in Genesis 11 (both J):

DIVINE DIALOGUE	
P	J
"Elokim said: 'Let US make man in our image and likeness.'" (Genesis 1:26)	"So Hashem-Elokim said: 'Behold, man has become like one of US . . .'" (Genesis 3:22) "Hashem said: 'They are a single people, all having one language—and this is what they have begun to do? So now, should they not be prevented from doing whatever they planned to do? Come, let US descend and confuse their speech there, so that one person will not understand another's speech.'" (Genesis 11:6–7)

Another parallel comes in the naming of creation. In chapter 1, God names the objects that are higher than and beyond man's control yet are subject to God's will (e.g., light, darkness, heaven, seas, and dry land). In chapter 2, man determines the names of the creatures he is given to dominate, namely the animals.

Finally, on every occasion that God creates something, He speaks and the Creation comes into being—with two exceptions. God inserts a sort of verbal drum roll to introduce His creation of man in Genesis 1 (supposedly written by P), and He does so again before introducing His creation of woman in Genesis 2 (supposedly written by J). Because of the special importance God attaches to these creations, He leads up to them with these statements:

| CREATION OF MAN AND WOMAN ||
P	J
"Let us make man . . ." (Genesis 1:26)	**"It is not good for man to be alone . . ."** (Genesis 2:18)

The Bible critics invented the "two accounts of creation" theory because they failed to notice the above parallels, which are the one author's method of linking ideas and themes throughout his book.

The Bible critics incessantly remind us that P likes laws and that E is a storyteller. Yet as the following example makes clear, when E wants to proclaim a law, his style is exactly that of P. The Bible's author has a highly idiosyncratic way of giving laws, beginning with a factual scenario ("When . . ."), then adding nuanced conditions ("if . . .") that result in different outcomes.

In this example, the Bible critics give the passage from Exodus to E because it concerns civil legislation, and they give the passage from Leviticus to P because it concerns ritual legislation. The Bible critics are so focused on these preconceived notions about their one-dimensional authors that they fail to see the tight parallels between these texts.

"When . . . If . . ."

E

"WHEN you buy a Hebrew servant, he shall labor for six years, and in the seventh he shall go out free, for nothing."

"IF he came in [to servitude] by himself, he shall leave by himself."

"IF he is married, his wife shall leave with him."

"IF his master gave him a wife and she bore him sons or daughters, the wife and her children will be her master's, and he will go out by himself."

"And IF the servant should say . . ." (Exodus 21:2–5)

P

"WHEN a person from among you brings a sacrifice to God, from the cattle—from the herd and from the flock—shall you bring your sacrifice."

"IF his sacrifice is a burnt offering . . ."

"And IF his sacrifice is from the flocks—from the sheep or from the goats, as a burnt offering . . ."

"And IF his burnt offering to God is from the birds . . ." (Leviticus 1:1–14)

Double-Talk

Double-talk is a rare stylistic pattern found in the Bible. The author will begin a sentence with something like "They said . . ." and then begin the next sentence with "They said . . ." From a literary standpoint, this writing style may at first blush seem repetitive, even juvenile. After all, we already know that the speaker is speaking. Why the double-talk?

Here are a few examples from J, E, and P:

DOUBLE-TALK		
J **Sodom & Gomorrah**	E **Joseph & Pharaoh**	P **Children of Gad & Reuben**
"**THEY SAID**: 'Stand back!' "**THEY SAID**: 'This fellow came to sojourn and would act as a judge? Now we will treat you worse than them.'" (Genesis 19:9)	*"PHARAOH SAID TO JOSEPH: 'Since God has made all this known to you, there is no one as discerning and wise as you. You shall be in charge of my court, and by your orders will all my people be provided for. Only by the throne will I outrank you.' "PHARAOH SAID TO JOSEPH: 'See! I have placed you in charge of all the land of Egypt.'" (Genesis 41:39–41)*	"The children of Reuben and children of Gad owned cattle in very great numbers. Noting that the lands of Jaezer and Gilead were a region suitable for cattle, the children of Gad and the children of Reuben came to Moses . . . AND SAID: 'Atarot, and Divon, and Jaezer, and Nimrah, and Heshbon, and El'aleh, and S'vam, and Nevo, and Veon . . . the land that Hashem has conquered for the community of Israel is cattle country, and your servants have cattle.' "THEY SAID: 'It would be a favor to us if this land were given to your servants as a holding; do not bring us across the Jordan.'" (Numbers 32:1–5)

Far from juvenile, the Bible's author employs this literary device in order to make readers think. Some nonverbal action has taken place between the first and second statements. The double-talk is the clue.

In the first example of Sodom and Gomorrah, the mob is trying to break down Lot's door to get at his guests. They say, "Stand back!" (Obviously, Lot did not.) So they continue: "Now we'll treat you (Lot) worse than the guests."

In the story of Joseph and Pharaoh, the erstwhile Hebrew

jailbird satisfactorily interprets the Egyptian monarch's dreams. Pharaoh says: "Since no one is wiser than you are, you are now viceroy of all Egypt, second only to me." (Joseph must be looking at Pharaoh as if he were an escaped mental patient. A despised foreigner was just hurried out of jail; now he is to be Egypt's ruler?) So Pharaoh says again, "I'm putting you in charge of the entire country!"

In our third example, the Children of Israel had just spent forty years wandering in the desert because they had badmouthed the good land that God was leading them to. Now after a generation of trials and tribulations, Moses and the children of Israel are just across the river from Israel, only steps away from their ultimate destination, when the tribes of Reuben and Gad say: "This land just outside of Israel is cattle country. We have cattle." (There was an icy silence, as Reuben and Gad did not get to hear what they had hoped Moses would say: "Wait a minute! I've got an idea. This is great land for cattle, and *you* have cattle. Perfect! Why don't you just keep this land!" Because they did not get the answer they wanted, they had to muster up the courage to ask for permission to stay on the periphery of the Land of Israel.) The tribes of Reuben and Gad then say, "We would be much obliged if we could remain in this land."

The double-talk is a clever and purposeful style choice made by the Bible's author. Failing to take note of the author's literary craft, the Bible critics went ahead and assigned the various texts to J, E, and P on the basis of superficial criteria.

Play on Words

"Punning occurs frequently, for example, in the texts known in scholarship as the sources J and E, but it is rare in the texts known as the sources P and D."[2]

The reason for this claim by Richard Elliott Friedman is fairly obvious. Punning is done in stories (which the critics assigned to J and E), not in legal (P) or historical (D) writing.

But as you can see from the examples below (more easily perhaps for those who have knowledge of the Hebrew language), J, E, P, and D all pun *the same*. In fact, in one instance, J and E make the exact same pun.

P

"In the beginning (*bereshit*) God created (*bara*) the heavens and the earth. The earth was astonishingly empty (*tohu vavohu*), with darkness upon the surface of the deep, and the Divine Presence (*ruach*) hovered (*merachefet*) upon the surface of the waters." (Genesis 1:1–2)

"Hashem said to Moses: 'Say to Aaron: Stretch (*neteh*) out your staff (*matchah*) and strike the dust of the land; it shall become lice throughout the land of Egypt.'" (Exodus 8:12)

"Do not count (*tifkod*) the tribe of Levi or take a census of them with the Israelites. You shall appoint (*hafked*) the Levites over the Mishkan . . ." (Numbers 1:49–50)

"He followed the Israelite man into the tent (*el-hakubah*) and pierced them both, the Israelite man and the woman into her stomach (*el-kavatah*) . . ." (Numbers 25:8)

J

"[Cain said:] **'Am I my brother's keeper (*achi anochi*)?' Then He said: "What have you done? The blood (*dam*) of your brother cries out to Me from the ground (*adamah*). . . . You shall become a vagrant (*nah*) and a wanderer (*nad*) on earth. . . ." Cain said to Hashem: '. . . I must become a vagrant (*nah*) and a wanderer (*nad*) on earth; whoever meets me will** kill me!' Hashem placed a mark upon Cain so that none that meet him (*motz'oh*) might kill him. Cain left (*va'yetze*) the presence of Hashem and settled in the land of Nod (like *nad*), east of Eden (like *nad* backwards)." (Genesis 4:9–16)

"Dan (*Dan*) will judge (*yadin*) his people. . . ."

"Gad (*Gad*) will recruit (*gedud*) a regiment (*yegudenu*) and it will retreat (*yagud*) on its heel." (Genesis 49:16, 19)

"But Noah (*No'ach*) found favor (*cheyn*) in the eyes of Hashem." (Genesis 6:8)

[Note: *No'ach* is *cheyn* backwards in Hebrew.]

"But Er (*Er*) Judah's firstborn, was evil (*ra*) in the eyes of Hashem." (Genesis 38:7)

[Note: *Er* is *ra* backwards in Hebrew.]

"They said to one another: 'Come, let us make bricks (*hava nilbena l'vaynim*) . . .'" and Hashem said, ". . . let us, then, go down and confound their speech (*hava nayrdah v'navlah*)." (Genesis 11:3–7)

"Abimelech, King of the Philistines, gazed down through the window and saw—Behold! Isaac (*Yitzchak*) was jesting (*metzachek*) with his wife Rebecca." (Genesis 26:8)

[Here J makes the pun; E makes the *same* pun in Genesis 21:8–9. See below.]

"But the waters of the deep (*eid*) went up from the earth and watered the whole face of the ground (*adamah*). Then Hashem Elokim formed the man (*adam*) of dust from the ground (*adamah*) . . ."[3] (Genesis 2:6–7)

[Here J makes the pun; E makes the *same* pun in Numbers 12:3; see below].

E

"Now the man Moses was exceedingly humble, more than any person (ha'adam) on the face of the earth (ha'adamah)!" (Numbers 12:3)

[Here E makes the pun; J makes the *same* pun in Genesis 2:6–7. See above.]

"Abraham made a great feast on the day Isaac (Yitzchak) was weaned. Sarah saw the son of Hagar . . . mocking (metzachek)." (Genesis 21:8–9)

[Here E makes the pun; J makes the *same* pun in Genesis 26:8. See above.]

"Laban overtook Jacob . . . (and) stationed himself on Mount Gilead (Gilad). . . . Laban said to Jacob: '. . . Let us make a covenant, I and you, and it should be a witness (l'eid) between me and you.'"

". . . Jacob said to his brethren: 'Gather stones!' So they took stones and made a mound (gal) . . . Laban called it Y'gar Sahadutah. But Jacob called it Gal-Eid ("mound of testimony.")" (Genesis 31:25–47)

"I have given you Shechem—one ("portion" = shechem) more than your brothers." (Genesis 48:22)

[Note: Jacob gives Joseph the double portion customarily given to the firstborn; he gives Joseph the territory around *Shechem*, which also means "portion."]

"When he saw the Kenites (kini) he proclaimed . . . 'You live in a fortress, and have placed your nest (knecha) in a cliff. . . .'" (Numbers 24:21)

D

"Because you trespassed against Me among the Children of Israel at the waters of Meribath-kadesh (merivat kadesh), in the wilderness of Zin; because you

did not sanctify (*kidashtem*) <u>Me among the Children of
Israel. . . . Hashem came from Sinai . . . and then approached
with some of the holy myriads</u> (*merivevot kodesh*) <u>. . .</u>."
(Deuteronomy 32:51, 33:2)

Although the Bible critics unfairly favor J and E in their story-
telling assignments, P and D do spin a few yarns and in so doing
manage to slip numerous puns past the Bible critics.

First Person / Third Person

The Bible's author assigns a unique style of speech to God
throughout the Bible. In the Bible, God sometimes begins a sentence in the first person but ends in the third person. Only God
speaks in this way—not Abraham, not Joseph, not Moses. So who
wrote all of God's parts when he switched from first to third person—J, E, P, or D? It turns out that although they lived in different
times and places, they all got the same memo. All four of the Bible's
alleged authors shift from first to third person when quoting God.

FIRST TO THIRD PERSON			
J	*E*	P	<u>D</u>
"For I have loved him (Abraham), because he commands his children and his household after him that they keep the way of HASHEM, doing charity and justice, in order that HASHEM might then bring upon Abraham that which He had spoken of him." (Genesis 18:19)[4]	*"And He (God) said: 'And this is the sign that I have sent you: When you take the people out of Egypt, you shall serve ELOKIM on this mountain.'"* (Exodus 3:12)[5]	"ELOKIM spoke all these statements, saying: 'I am HASHEM, your God, who has taken you out of the land of Egypt, from the house of bondage. You shall have no other gods in my presence. . . . You shall not take the Name of HASHEM, your God, in vain, for Hashem will not absolve anyone who takes His Name in vain.'" (Exodus 20:1–7)[6]	<u>"HASHEM swore: '. . . Except for Caleb . . . He shall see it, and to him shall I give the Land on which he walked, and to his children, because he followed HASHEM wholeheartedly.'"</u> (Deuteronomy 1:36)[7]

Cliffhangers

The Bible's author, like many a good suspense writer, will inject a comforting thought and then hit the reader with a jarring conclusion. Had the Bible critics noticed this style, they might have avoided apportioning examples of this among J, E, and P.

CLIFFHANGERS		
J	E	P
"He also married Rachel, and he also loved Rachel— more than Leah." (Genesis 29:30)	*"Within three days Pharaoh will lift up your head—and restore you to your position."* (Genesis 40:13) *"Within three days Pharaoh will lift up your head—from the rest of you; he will hang you on a tree."* (Genesis 40:19)	"And the magicians did so with their secret arts (and were successful)." (Exodus 7:22; 8:3) "And the magicians did so with their secret arts to bring forth the lice—but they could not!" (Exodus 8:14)

Some very pious people have difficulty with the idea that the Bible's author had a sense of humor. Yet the above verses seem to indicate that he did. Whatever the case may be, each of these cliffhangers sets the stage for the pivotal events that follow:

1. Jacob's greater love for Rachel leads to jealousy among the next generation, which leads to Joseph's exile in Egypt;
2. Joseph's ability to interpret dreams leads to his position as viceroy under Pharaoh; and
3. The inability of Pharaoh's magicians to match God's power sets the stage for God's victory over Pharaoh and the exodus from Egypt.

Dreams

In the Bible, dreams exist only in pairs. Joseph had two dreams; Pharaoh had two dreams; and the baker's and butler's dreams were paired while they served jail time with Joseph. Both J and E appear to have shared this notion that dreams always come in twos.

TWO SETS OF DREAMS	
J	E
Joseph (Genesis 37)	*Baker and Butler* (Genesis 40) *Pharaoh* (Genesis 41)

The Third Day

J and E may dream about doubles, but they obsess about triples:

THE THIRD DAY	
J	E
"And it came to pass on the THIRD DAY, when they were in pain . . ." (Genesis 34:25) **". . . He herded them into a ward for a three-day period. Joseph said to them on the THIRD DAY . . ."** (Genesis 42:17–18) **"Let them be prepared for the THIRD DAY, for on the THIRD DAY Hashem shall descend . . . on Mount Sinai. . . ."** (Exodus 19:11)	*"On the THIRD DAY, Abraham raised his eyes and perceived the place from afar."* (Genesis 22:4) *"It was told to Laban on the THIRD DAY that Jacob had fled."* (Genesis 31:22) *"And it was on the THIRD DAY, Pharaoh's birthday . . ."* (Genesis 40:20)

Forty

J, E, and P all share a fetish for 40 (and multiples thereof); the completion of a cycle of 40 (or 400) always brings something new:

FORTY		
J	**E**	**P**
Flood (40 Days) Israelites' Exile in Egypt (400 Years)	Moses' Stay on Mount Sinai (40 Days)	Twelve Spies' Journey to Canaan (40 Days) Israelites' Stay in the Desert (40 Years)

The Flood cleansed the world of a corrupt generation, allowing a fresh start for Noah and his family; the Egyptian exile transformed Israel from a clan to a nation; Moses goes up the mountain and comes down with the Torah; the spies journey to Canaan to bring evidence of the greatness of their new country; the Israelites prolong their stay in the desert to allow the older generation to die so that a new generation, one that is born in freedom, will be able to wage war and conquer Canaan.

The Younger Prevails over the Older

The stifling conformity of the Bible's authors makes it harder and harder to tell them apart. J, E, P, and D consistently identify one's baby brother as more worthy:

THE ELDER & YOUNGER		
SOURCE	**ELDER**	**YOUNGER**
J	Cain	Abel
J	Japheth	Shem
E-P	Ishmael	Isaac
J	Esau	Jacob
J-E	The Brothers	Joseph
J	Er, Onan	Shela
J	Zerah	Perez
E	Menasseh	Ephraim
J-P	Miriam, Aaron	Moses
P	Gershon, Merari	Kohath
P	Nadab, Abihu	Elazar, Ithamar
P	The Firstborn	Levites
D	The Nations	Israel

Unique Terminology

We have looked at several examples (there are many more) of the Bible's unique literary style crossing the pseudo-boundaries erected by the Bible critics. But beyond literary style, we present here unique terminology that also cuts across the Bible critics' division of sources. In other words, we are not looking at ordinary words that one might expect to see in use by different people, but at unique phrases that one would not expect different authors to use. There are countless examples throughout the Bible; here are just a few of them:

"GO ON YOUR WAY . . ."		
J	E	P
"Hashem said to Abram: 'GO ON YOUR WAY . . . from your land, from your relatives, and from your father's house to the land that I will show you.'" (Genesis 12:1)	*"God tested Abraham, and said to him: 'Abraham . . . Please take your son, Isaac, and GO ON YOUR WAY . . . to the land of Moriah; bring him up there as an offering upon one of the mountains which I shall tell you.'"* (Genesis 22:1–2)	"Hashem spoke to Moses, saying: 'SEND ON THEIR WAY . . . men, and let them spy out the land . . .'" (Numbers 13:1–2)

Hebrew speakers use the imperative form of a verb just as English speakers do: "Go!" "Send!" But in a few instances, the unusual reflexive phrasing "on your way" (or awkwardly, but more literally, "for you") follows the verb.[8] Because of the way the Bible critics have sliced and diced the Bible, this unique terminology gets *apportioned among three of their sources.*

"Am I instead of God?" is a unique phrase that occurs only twice in the Bible. Like father like son, Joseph utters a phrase introduced by his father Jacob. The uniqueness was lost on the Bible critics, who assign these parts to E and J. (Perhaps the hypothesized biblical authors E and J were father and son?)

| "AM I INSTEAD OF GOD?" ||
E	J
"Rachel saw that she had not borne children to Jacob, so Rachel became envious of her sister; she said to Jacob: 'Give me children—Otherwise I am dead.' Jacob's anger flared up at Rachel, and he said: 'AM I INSTEAD OF GOD who has withheld from you fruit of the womb?'" (Genesis 30:1–2)	**"His brothers . . . went and flung themselves before him and said: 'We are ready to be your slaves.' But Joseph said to them: 'Fear not, for AM I INSTEAD OF GOD. . . . ?'"** (Genesis 50:18–20)

The two verses below are just three chapters apart, but E and J have a habit of completing each other's thoughts. Here each tells a part of the same story, using a phrase one would not expect to recur between different authors:

| "GOOD IN PHARAOH'S EYES" ||
E	J
"The matter appeared good in Pharaoh's eyes and in the eyes of all his servants." (Genesis 41:37)	**"The news was heard in Pharaoh's palace . . . and it was good in Pharaoh's eyes and in the eyes of his servants."** (Genesis 45:16)

The Bible's author has a characteristic way of stating something in both the affirmative and the negative. In carving up the Bible, the Bible critics parceled "remember" and "do not forget" between both E and D:

REMEMBER AND DO NOT FORGET		
_E_	D	D
"Yet the Chamberlain of the Cupbearers did not REMEMBER Joseph, but he FORGOT him." (Genesis 40:23)	"REMEMBER what Amalek did to you . . . you shall wipe out the memory of Amalek . . . you shall not FORGET!" (Deuteronomy 25:17–19)	"REMEMBER, do not FORGET, that you provoked Hashem, your God, in the Wilderness . . ." (Deuteronomy 9:7)

The Bible's author artfully uses a unique phrase—"for all who come [or 'depart'] through the gate of his city"—in two stories that have much in common: Abraham's purchase of a burial plot for his wife Sarah and his grandson Jacob's encounter with the people of Shechem. Both stories involve interactions with the local Canaanite population; both involve the townspeople acting as witnesses; both involve land purchases; both involve Canaanite deception; both revolve around female misfortune (the death of Sarah and the rape of Dinah); and both include invitations to join the local population.

In the case of Shechem, the price of becoming one people is male circumcision, which is why the Bible's author puts a humorous twist on the unique phrase marking these bookends: "for all who _depart_ through the gate of his city." Apparently, the townspeople were all heading for the exit when they learned the requirements of Israelite citizenship. The phrase is unique, the stories are uniquely related, but the Bible critics divide the portions between P and J (and give an earlier part of the story regarding the purchase of land in Shechem to E).[9]

FROM HEBRON TO SHECHEM	
P	J
". . . for all who come through the gate of his city . . ." (Genesis 23:10 & 18)	". . . for all who depart through the gate of his city . . ." (Genesis 34:24)

Conclusion

The Bible critics have long claimed to find different biblical authors based on differences in style. But the differences they highlight are not persuasive. To distinguish between E and P because one tells stories and the other proclaims rules is as silly as saying that a father is actually two different people because at night he reads his young son a bedtime story but during the day he lays down the law when his son misbehaves.

Far more powerful are the unities, the deliberate parallelism of style and terminology across the passages claimed for the critics' alphabet of authors. To account for these powerful parallels the Bible critics have nothing to fall back on but the alleged editor R, who can turn any failure of the theory into a triumph. But if R can do that then he *is* the single author of the Bible, and the Bible critics nullify their own multiple-author theory.

The Bible critics are aware of at least some of the striking similarities we have shown in this chapter. Even Robert Alter has commented, "I should add that efforts to distinguish between J and E on stylistic grounds have been quite unconvincing."[10]

So much so that Richard Elliot Friedman writes: "The question remains as to why so many similarities exist between J and E. They often tell similar stories. They deal largely with the same characters. They share much terminology. Their styles are sufficiently similar that it has never been possible to separate them on stylistic grounds alone."[11]

Yet his answer reflects a deep state of denial:

"One possible explanation of this is that one of them is based on the other. . . . They would still be drawing upon a common treasury of history and tradition . . . biblical in style as well, once one version was established as a document bearing sacred national traditions, the author of the second, alternate version might well have consciously (or perhaps even unconsciously) decided to imitate its style."[12]

So J and E are so similar that we cannot know where one begins and where the other ends (but they're going to tell us anyway).

Friedman continues with his explanation: "Another possible explanation for the stylistic similarity of J and E is that, rather than J's being based on E or E's being based on J, *both* may have been based on a common source that was prior to them. That is, there may have been an old, traditional cycle of stories about the patriarchs, Exodus, etc., which both the authors of J and E used as a basis for their works."[13]

Why not simply say that what we have in front of us is the original source, and J and E are no more than a figment of the Bible critics' imagination? If you see identical twins, you can assume a common parent. The identical and purposely parallel literary style and unique terminology found throughout the Bible likewise imply a common author.

CHAPTER NINE

The Bible Critics' Tunnel Vision

Ideological blinders keep them from understanding the Bible

The Bible is not Mother Goose. It is an adult work of unparalleled depth.

Employing a variety of literary techniques, the author builds various tensions into a story whose later resolution is typically underscored through distinct parallels of language and theme. The author rewards attentive readers with a higher understanding of how man should live in the world. That is the author's purpose throughout the Bible.

The Bible critics thwart this purpose by dividing the Bible into imaginary sources, as if four independent writers with differing, even opposing perspectives could produce such unified stories.

Imagine trying to appreciate the Sistine Chapel from the premise that four artists—R(ed), G(reen), B(lue), and Y(ellow)—were responsible for that great work, which was only touched up by T; surely we would miss Michelangelo's vision.

And so it is with the Bible critics. They are so fixated on certain minutiae of importance to them—whether it be the presumed political interests of Aaron's descendants or the variant uses of the Divine name—that they are blind to the true meaning of the story.

To shed light on their tunnel vision, we will look at just five stories that any ordinary person who reads the Bible in a straight-forward fashion—in other words, with the understanding that later developments depend on ideas the author planted earlier on—should be able to comprehend.

The Nature of Man

One question that emerges in the very beginning of Genesis involves God's opinion of man. In the first few lines of the Bible, God pronounces judgment on his creations. First God creates light, then "God saw that the light was good."

God separates the earth from the seas. "And God saw that it was good."

He made fruit-bearing trees. "And God saw that it was good."

Sun, moon, and stars. "And God saw that it was good."

Fish and fowl. "And God saw that it was good."

Land animals. "And God saw that it was good."

Finally, comes man, and . . . no comment.

"AND GOD SAW THAT IT WAS GOOD" (P)	
DAY	**CREATION IS GOOD**
1	"God saw that the light was GOOD." (1:4)
3	"God called to the dry land "Earth," and to the gathering of waters He called 'Seas.' And God saw that it was GOOD." (1:10)
3	"And the earth brought forth vegetation, herbage yielding seed after its kind, and trees yielding fruit, each containing its seed after its kind. And God saw that it was GOOD." (1:12)
4	"And God set them in the firmament of the heaven to give light upon the earth, to dominate by day and by night, and to separate between the light and the darkness. And God saw that it was GOOD." (1:17–18)
5	"And God created the great sea-giants and every living being that creeps, with which the waters teemed after their kinds; and all winged fowl of every kind. And God saw that it was GOOD." (1:21)
6	"God made the beast of the earth according to its kind, and the animal according to its kind, and every creeping being of the ground according to its kind. And God saw that it was GOOD." (1:25)
6	"And God said, 'Let us make Man in Our image, after Our likeness . . .'" (1:26–28)
6	"And God saw all that He had made, and behold it was very GOOD." (1:31)

Clearly mankind is the pinnacle in this ascending order of creation since God gives man dominion over everything else. Yet it is a little discomfiting not hearing those words of confirmation.

Imagine an awards banquet where the Master of Ceremonies is hosting seven honorees. As each receives praise from his host, the next honoree awaits his turn in joyful anticipation. Finally, it is the seventh honoree's turn. The host notes the importance of his role, yet gives him no positive feedback. At the conclusion of the banquet, the host offers a collective pat on the back—but still no comment about the seventh honoree individually.

This is what happens in Genesis 1. Its last verse states, "And God saw all that He had made, and behold it was very good . . ."

What would you conclude if you had been passed over at such a banquet? One reasonable inference would be that though your task is of surpassing importance, you have yet to prove yourself.

That is what the Bible's author appears to be saying. Man is different from the other creations. Man has free choice. God is reserving judgment until he sees what man makes of his freedom. The first test comes in the Garden of Eden. God tells man he may eat of any tree except for the Tree of Knowledge of Good and Bad.

As we all know, Adam and Eve fail that first test of freedom. Next, jealous Cain takes his brother Abel's life. By the time we get to Noah, the world situation under man's dominion of the earth has declined precipitously. Rapacious rulers are taking any woman that pleases them; the mighty are oppressing the weak.

In ten generations of observation, God sees increasing violence and sexual depravity. Man has failed the test. After leaving us hanging in Genesis 1, the Bible's author gives us God's judgment:

Hashem saw that the wickedness of Man was great upon the earth, and that every product of the thoughts of his heart was but **evil** always. (Genesis 6:5)

After teasing us in chapter 1, the author relieves our suspense in chapter 6, having shown the erosion of man's character in between. Taken as a coherent whole, it should be obvious what the author is saying: that God's first experiment in human freedom was a big disappointment. This is confirmed when God brings a flood to destroy all flesh, except for Noah, his family, and their menagerie of pets.

The author even took pains to underline this theme with unique verbal cues. Normally, one pronounces judgment through speech. But the Bible's author gets readers' attention in an unusual way. In every case in Genesis 1, God *saw* that his creation was good. And so, too, in chapter 6: God *saw* the wickedness of man. Is man good? See for yourself:

IS MAN GOOD?	
P	J
"And God SAW that it was GOOD . . ." (Genesis 1:4, 10, 12, 18, 21, 25, 31)	"And Hashem SAW that the wickedness of Man was great upon the earth, and that every product of the thoughts of his heart was but EVIL always." (Genesis 6:5)

This story about the ascending order of creation and the descending moral state of man is perfectly coherent. Yet because the Bible critics give Genesis 1 to P and the next several chapters to J, they fail to see the unity of theme and unity of language that give this story its narrative power.

FROM GENESIS TO THE FLOOD	
EPISODE	SOURCE
Creation (Genesis 1)	P
Garden of Eden and the Fall of Man (Genesis 2–3)	J
First Brothers—First Murder (Genesis 4)	J
The First Civilization—Power and Violence (Genesis 4)	J
Unraveling of the Generations from Creation (Genesis 5)	P or R
Utter Corruption of these Generations (Genesis 6:1–4)	J
Conclusion: Man is Evil (Genesis 6:5)	J

Note that a consensus of the Bible critics claims J was written well before P. How could J deliver the moral of a story that P would only set up many centuries afterward?

Who Gets the Blessing? The Story of Jacob and Esau

Another famous Bible story centers on the drama of which son, Jacob or Esau, will receive his blind father Isaac's blessing.

Recall that while Esau was out hunting game, Jacob was using his brother's name. "It is I, Esau your firstborn," said Jacob, who smelled like his brother and felt like his brother because of a masterful deception engineered by his mother Rebecca.

Isaac eats of the delicacies prepared by Rebecca and blesses Jacob:

> And may God give you of the dew of the heavens and of the fatness of the earth, and abundant grain and wine. Peoples will serve you, and regimes will prostrate themselves to you; be a lord to your kinsmen, and your mother's sons will prostrate themselves to you . . . (Genesis 27:28–29)

No sooner than Isaac completes the blessing and Jacob leaves the tent, Esau returns with his freshly prepared meat, asking for his blessing. Isaac trembles in confusion, but declares the blessing irrevocable. Esau bitterly cries, "Bless me, too, Father!"

But Isaac said, "Your brother came with cleverness and took your blessing." (Genesis 27:35)

Jacob flees to his uncle, Laban, leaving his home, his parents, and the land of Canaan, fearful that Esau would kill him.

Fast-forward two decades. Jacob had worked for twenty years in a foreign land for the swindler Laban, who constantly changed the terms of their wage exchanges. In his most infamous deception, Laban gave his daughter Leah to Jacob for a bride when Jacob had purposely labored seven years for Leah's younger sister, Rachel.

Now, after many hardships, including his flight back to Canaan with Laban and his kinsmen in hot pursuit, Jacob sends emissaries to Esau in "the land of Seir, the field of Edom," with a message of his arrival.

Jacob's behavior is baffling. After two difficult decades trying to escape his brother's wrath, does he really have to say, "Yoo-hoo, guess who's coming to dinner?"—especially when his brother is in Seir, which lies outside of Canaan?

Predictably, the very next thing we learn is that the emissaries return saying that Esau "is coming toward you, and four hundred men are with him." This is not a greeting party; it's an army out to kill. Frightened, Jacob divides his people into two camps, figuring at least one will survive if Esau attacks. He then tries to appease his brother with a massive tribute. He has his servants bring vast flocks and herds, each drove separated by a great distance, so that Esau is continually surprised by the generosity of the gift.

Then the encounter. Seeing Esau and his army, Jacob divides his children, goes ahead of them, and bows seven times until reaching Esau.

"Esau ran toward him, embraced him, fell upon his neck, and kissed him; then they wept." (Genesis 33:4)

The appeasement works. Next, Esau inquires about Jacob's wives and children, who bow to Esau. Then they discuss the tribute, Esau magnanimously telling Jacob to keep his offering. Jacob begs Esau to accept his gift:

"Please take my blessing which was brought to you, inasmuch as God has been gracious to me and inasmuch as I have everything." He urged him, and he accepted. (Genesis 33:11)

A beautiful reconciliation, and at last we can understand Jacob's encounter with his brother. As usual, the Bible's author hints at it through verbal cues. Jacob does not say, "Accept my gift," as you might expect.[1] He says "take" (*kach* in Hebrew) "my blessing" (*birchati* in Hebrew), just as earlier Isaac had told Esau that his brother "took" (*vayikach*) "your blessing" (*birchatecha*).

Jacob's objective was to atone for his earlier deception in taking his brother's blessing: I took your blessing, now you take mine. And he carried out this "make-good" with exactitude. Isaac's blessing included the "fatness of the earth," and, indeed, despite all his hardships, Jacob was now a wealthy man. And he transferred that wealth to his brother by droves.

Isaac's blessing also included familial supremacy: "be a lord to your kinsmen, and your mother's sons will prostrate themselves to you." Jacob constantly refers to his brother as "my lord," to himself as "your servant," and he and his wives and children bow down to Esau.

Before he arranges this encounter, Jacob the deceiver spends twenty years in the deception capital of the world, with his uncle (and father-in-law), Laban.

So we come full-circle, quite literally, as Jacob flees (from Esau) to the land of his uncle, Laban, outside of Israel, then ends up fleeing Laban (and encountering Esau) on his way back to Israel.

This is a story of deception and destiny, exile and return, reconciliation and repentance. It is a tightly woven unitary narrative with rich parallels of language and plot, which we have only skimmed. The Bible critics take this beautiful literary construction and rip it to shreds by assigning the first part of the story to J and all of the beautiful and precise parallels to E.

JACOB TAKES & RETURNS THE BLESSING	
J	E
"Your brother came with cleverness and took your blessing." (Genesis 27:35)	*"Please, take my blessing . . ."* (Genesis 33:11)

Gateway to Freedom

One seemingly quirky law in the book of Exodus concerns the treatment of a Hebrew bondsman who does not wish to be set free. He is brought to a doorpost and a hole is made in his ear.

Besides the oddness of this ritual, it seems inhumane. But the laws of a Hebrew slave, as distinct from the kind of chattel slavery that readers are familiar with from U.S. and world history, are anything but inhumane.

The Hebrew justice system was based on restitution, not incarceration. If a thief lacked the means to make restitution, or if a debtor were bankrupt, he would pay off his debt with his labor.

But there were limitations on this kind of indentured servitude, the primary one being the term of service. A slave could not work beyond six years. No matter how great the value of his theft, biblical law compelled a master to release his servant in the seventh year. But the next verse is a little puzzling:

> But if the bondsman shall say, "I love my master, my wife, and my children—I shall not go free," then his master shall bring him to the court and shall bring him to the door or to the doorpost, and his master shall bore through his ear with the awl, and he shall serve him forever. (Exodus 21:5–6)

How are we to explain this strange biblical command? The answer, found just a few chapters earlier (Exodus 12:7, 22–23), explains the seeming oddity of the ritual and elucidates the humanity of biblical values.

These verses describe another ritual involving a doorpost. God is about to execute the tenth plague, striking the firstborn of the Egyptians but passing over the Hebrews' homes containing the blood of a lamb brushed onto the doorposts, a pre-arranged sign.

The connection between Exodus 12 and Exodus 21 should be fairly obvious: it's all part of the same story. Both deal with doorposts and both deal with slavery. The original doorpost ritual was the last step before God brought the Children of Israel out of Egypt. That doorpost was the gateway to freedom. For a Hebrew slave to beg to remain a slave not only denies his own freedom, but the Exodus itself.

Man was created to serve God, not to serve other men who oppress their slaves. As with so much of the Bible, symbols and rituals are employed to internalize its ideas about the purpose of man's existence.

This ear-piercing ceremony is also a commentary on the prevailing gentile law of the time, which was to cut off the ear of a slave who denied he was a slave. (The Code of Hammurabi, for example, says: "If a slave says to his master: 'You are not my master,' if they convict him his master shall cut off his ear.") So biblical law is diametrically opposite. His ear is pierced—not cut off—if he does *not* want to go free, as if to say, "Your ear didn't hear the message: freedom is the desired state of mankind."

This story is as compelling as it is coherent. If read continuously and as a whole, its meaning is apparent. But that is not how the Bible critics read the Bible, and hence they are unable to hear what the Bible's author is saying loud and clear. In their source division, it is E who writes the law of the slave taken to the doorpost, and P and J who write different bits of the paschal lamb and doorpost scenes.

DOORPOST	
E	P-J
"The slave is taken to the doorpost." (Exodus 21:6)	**Paschal lamb—The doorpost** (Exodus 12:7—P); (Exodus 12:22–23—J)[2]

Paradise Lost?

A story that has preoccupied Bible readers from early churchmen to modern archeologists has been the location of the Garden of Eden. The book of Genesis provides tantalizing clues: It is a place where a river divides into four branches, two of which are the well-known Tigris and Euphrates rivers; although we don't know exactly where the Pishon and Gihon rivers are, we are told that the former encircles a land where one can find gold, *bedolach,* and the *shoham* stone; the latter is said to encircle Cush, traditionally thought to be Ethiopia.

Opinions on the garden's location vary enormously. Most look to ancient Mesopotamia; some have claimed that Iranian Azerbaijan or Ethiopia best match biblical clues; some religious believers say that modern geography differs from antediluvian times and that therefore the Garden of Eden exists exactly as described, but in Independence, Missouri, Bristol, Florida, or more exotic locations, such as Java or the Seychelles islands.

But maybe these Eden quests are missing the point. After all, the author says that God drove man out of the garden. What's more, God seems to have shut the door, as it were, on physically re-entering:

"And having driven out the man, He stationed at the east of the Garden of Eden the Cherubim and the flame of the ever-turning sword, to guard the way to the Tree of Life." (Genesis 3:24)

So we know that entrance from the eastern end is impossible because man cannot get past the flame of the ever-turning sword. Is there another way in?

Quite possibly. Eden is no longer a biblical subject after Genesis 4, and there is no reappearance of an ever-turning sword or Tree of Life. But we do again encounter the Cherubim. In the book of Exodus, after God gives the Children of Israel the Ten

Commandments, they are to build an ark (at the west end of the Tabernacle) to encase the tablets. Upon the ark are to be two winged Cherubim made of gold.

We only need look at their earlier appearance in Genesis 3:24 to understand what these Cherubim stand for. They guard the way to the Tree of Life in the Garden of Eden. (And just as man is exiled east of Eden, similarly the Bible shows access to the Tabernacle to be from the east.)

In both cases, the Cherubim are guarding something precious. The Bible appears to be suggesting that the eternal life that was lost in Eden was restored to humanity when God gave the Torah at Sinai. The Torah containing God's commandments is itself a Tree of Life.

Does the text support this interpretation? Clearly the Cherubim mentioned in Exodus are more than just decoration. God Himself says that whenever He conducts business with Moses, it will be from between those two Cherubim that He will issue His commands.

> . . . into the Ark shall you place the Testimonial tablets that I shall give you. It is there that I will set My meetings with you, and I shall speak with you from atop the Cover, from between the two Cherubim that are on the Ark of the Testimonial tablets, everything that I shall command you to the Children of Israel. (Exodus 25:21–22)

And in many places in the Bible the Children of Israel are told that following God's commands will bring blessings and that failing to do so will bring curses. The former is explicitly linked to life, as in the lost Tree of Life:

> See—I have placed before you today the life and the good, and the death and the evil. That which I command you

today, to love Hashem, your God, to walk in His ways, to observe His commandments, His decrees, and His ordinances; then you will live and you will multiply, and Hashem, your God, will bless you in the Land to which you come, to possess it. (Deuteronomy 30:15–16)

The Bible's author seems to be saying that there is indeed a way back into the Garden of Eden, and the path lies through the observance of God's commandments. As for the threatening swords in the way, they are not barriers to Israel's peace in the land God promised His people. Moses' final blessing at the end of Deuteronomy makes clear that when Israel accepts the yoke of Torah, God will vanquish its enemies, and he says so in language that parallels the Garden of Eden:

"He drove the enemy away from before you, and He said, 'Destroy!' Thus Israel shall dwell secure . . ." (Deuteronomy 33:27–28)

So just as God drove man out (*vaygaresh* in Hebrew) of the garden and stationed (*vayishkon*) Cherubim, so, too, will God drive away (*vaygaresh*) Israel's enemies, allowing Israel to dwell (*vayishkon*) in tranquility.

THE GARDEN OF EDEN	THE LAND OF ISRAEL
J	D
"And having driven the man (*vaygaresh*), He stationed (*vayashken*—literally, 'caused to dwell') **at the east of the Garden of Eden the Cherubim . . . to guard the path to the Tree of Life."** (Genesis 3:24)	"He drove (*vaygaresh*) the enemy away from before you, and He said: 'Destroy!' Thus Israel shall dwell (*vayishkon*) secure . . ." (Deuteronomy 33:27–28)

The very beginning of the Torah shows that man lost an ideal existence of tranquility and immortality, and the very end of the Torah, in typical bookend fashion, holds forth the possibility of reclaiming that ideal existence.

CHERUBIM	
J	P
Guard the Garden of Eden	Guard the Tablets

So all is not lost. According to the Bible's author, we can almost enter Eden again if we but keep God's commandments. Man need not despair over a lost paradise. A more ideal existence, full of life and blessing, is within anyone's reach.

Alas, this thread, which not only links the Bible from beginning to end but also constitutes its primary message, is deconstructed out of existence by Bible critics who give the Eden Cherubim to J, the Ark Cherubim to P, and the moral of the story at the end of the Torah to D.

God's Attributes

We've looked at the nature of man, but what about the nature of God? Just what kind of characteristics does He possess? Is He a God of compassion who can forgive a big sin, such as the idolatry of the Golden Calf? Or is He a God of strict justice who would expel man from the Garden of Eden for eating a forbidden piece of fruit?

We have already looked at the Expulsion from the Garden of Eden; let's look at the Golden Calf story.

God had just brought a nation of slaves out of bondage. He guided the people to a land He had promised their ancestors; He provided food for them to eat (manna) and water for them to drink; as a special bonus He offered them a covenant at Sinai. In other words, He was not merely redeeming a promise to Israel's ancestors. Rather, He revealed himself to the multitude of Abraham's, Isaac's, and Jacob's descendants and offered to make them His treasured people and a holy nation if they would accept His law. The people enthusiastically agreed.

One of God's conditions—stated in the second commandment—was loyalty:

You shall not make yourself a carved image nor any likeness of that which is in the heavens above or on the earth below or in the water beneath the earth. (Exodus 20:4)

Failure to adhere to this commitment was to be dealt with strictly, as the next verse states:

You shall not prostrate yourself to them nor worship them, for I am Hashem, your God—a jealous God, Who visits the sin of fathers upon children to the third and fourth generations, for My enemies. (Exodus 20:5)

And loyalty is rewarded per the next verse:
". . . but Who shows kindness for thousands [of generations] to those who love Me and observe My commandments." (Exodus 20:6)

The next verse is the third commandment, where God again shows His strict side to those who would tarnish His reputation:
". . . for Hashem will not absolve anyone who takes His Name in vain." (Exodus 20:7)

God reinforces this strictness after giving the people laws, when He appoints an angel to guide them on their way:

". . . do not rebel against him, for he will not forgive your willful sin—for My Name is within him." (Exodus 23:21)

As is well known, just as God and Moses were up on Sinai inking the deal (or rather setting it in stone), the people lost faith that Moses would ever return. On Moses' fortieth day on the mountain, the people violated the second and third commandments to which they had agreed. They made for themselves an idolatrous image and in the process sullied the reputation of the God who had liberated them from Egypt.

After all of His many kindnesses, this is the thanks He gets? Understandably, God wanted to take His wrath out on Israel and start all over again with Moses' family:

". . . Let My anger flare up against them and I shall annihilate them; and I shall make you a great nation." (Exodus 32:10)

Fortunately for Israel, Moses intercedes with God. The strength of God's relationship with Moses ("Hashem would speak to Moses . . . as a man would speak with his fellow . . ." [Exodus 33:11]) and the clever arguments that Moses advances save Israel. It helped, too, that Moses killed three thousand of the worst offenders and that God sent a plague to kill the other instigators.

But how do they move on from there? Even those who did not lead the idolatry were complicit in it. In Moses' merit, God agrees to repair relations with Israel and tells Moses to carve two new stone tablets for use as a new covenant.

But what will make this new covenant fare any better than the old one? After all, the nation of Israel is no less apt to err. Answer: it is God himself who establishes a new leniency. He will no longer judge His people as strictly as in the past but will instead bestow a level of mercy of which God alone is capable. He reveals these Divine attributes to Moses:

Hashem, Hashem, God, Compassionate and Gracious,

Slow to Anger, and Abundant in Kindness and Truth. Preserver of Kindness for thousands of generations, Forgiver of Iniquity, Willful Sin, and Error, and who Absolves—but does not absolve completely, remembering the sins of the fathers to their children and grandchildren, to the third and fourth generations. (Exodus 34:6–7)

Not only do God's attributes of mercy make a relationship possible between a perfect God and an unworthy people, but in his characteristic literary brilliance the Bible's author parallels the language of strictness found earlier in the story with a new perspective that perfectly resolves all the tension. The law of the Ten Commandments remains the same—the covenant is simply amended with mercy:

A "jealous God" is now a "merciful and forgiving God." An "angry God" is now "slow to anger." A God kind only to those who observe His commandments is now "abundant in kindness and truth." The God who would "not forgive willful sins" is now a "forgiver of willful sins." The God who would never "absolve" will now do so at His discretion. And the God who remembers the sins of the fathers upon children "for My enemies" no longer equates sinners with enemies. People sin out of weakness, not necessarily because they hate God. At the time of the sin of the Golden Calf, God wanted to wipe everyone out. The new view seems to be that there will be consequences for sin, but that sinners are tolerated to a degree.[3]

THE TWO COVENANTS AT SINAI	
P-*E* **ORIGINAL ATTRIBUTES**	**J** **ATTRIBUTES OF MERCY** **(EXODUS 34:6–7)**
"For I am . . . a jealous God" (Exodus 20:5—P)	**"Hashem, Hashem, a merciful and forgiving God"**
"Let My anger flare up against them" (Exodus 32:10—E)	**"Slow to anger"**
"Who shows kindness . . . to those who love Me and observe My commandments" (Exodus 20:6—P)	**"Abundant in kindness and truth"**
"Who shows kindness for thousands (of generations) to those who love Me and observe My commandments" (Exodus 20:6—P)	**"Preserves kindness for thousands** [of generations]**"**
". . . will not forgive your willful sins" (Exodus 23:21—E)	**"Forgiver of iniquity and willful sins"**
"For Hashem will not absolve" (Exodus 20:7—P)	**"Who cleanses, but does not cleanse completely"**
"Who remembers the sins of the fathers to their children to the third and fourth generations, for My enemies" (Exodus 20:5—P)	**"Who remembers the sins of the fathers to their children and grandchildren to the third and fourth generations"**

It turns out that God is a God of justice *and* mercy. Because of some very special people, Abraham, Isaac, Jacob, and Moses, God developed a very special relationship with the nation of Israel, a relationship that can survive many stresses.

This is a profound story about sin and redemption, about a relationship betrayed and repaired, about an early falling out and coming together that enabled the relationship to endure through many more tests. But the Bible critics, who credit J with the attributes of mercy and divide the original attributes between P and E, take the sublime and make it ridiculous. Remember, in their scheme, J, who stresses mercy, came first. So how does J transform the attributes of God, which were supposedly written by E and P, if J lived before E and P? The Bible critics' anachronistic division destroys this powerful tale of a relationship renewed and crushes the hope it creates.

• • •

We have looked at just five Bible stories, the resolution of which takes us on a zigzagging course through fragments of J, E, P, and D. Sometimes P sets up a tension that J will climactically resolve (the nature of man), absurdly, since J is supposed to have lived centuries before P. Sometimes J will sow an idea that E will later harvest (Jacob, Esau, and the blessing). Sometimes P and J sow the same seed, which E then harvests (the doorpost). Sometimes D serves as a bookend to J, while P inserts himself in the middle (expulsion and return to the Garden of Eden). And sometimes J is the mirror image reflecting the light of ideas emitted separately by E and P (attributes of God)—again, anachronistically.

In every case, the Bible's author crafted a story that imparts deep ideas about the human condition, and the Bible critics—because of their tunnel-vision commitment to certain preconceived ideas—demonstrate an inability to comprehend the story.

CHAPTER TEN

Intellectual Laziness

An unenergetic approach fails to yield results

A great author challenges his readers to think. And a great reader accepts that challenge by engaging the text, searching out a higher understanding.

The simple reader does not struggle with a text, but skims its surface, taking away a basic story line without any deeper layers of meaning. There is nothing especially wrong with that. If the book is well written, the reader will at least get something out of it.

Beyond the active reader and the simple one is the ideological reader. Like secular or religious dogmatists, the Bible critics already *have* the answers and consequently fail to engage the text even at the level of the simple reader. Like Soviet leaders who actually believed what they were reading in *Pravda*, and who were therefore quite surprised to finally learn that their society could not withstand competition with the West, the professional Bible critics' flaccid habits of mind poorly prepare them to teach, explain, or understand the Bible.

The Bible critics are ever alert to find text-based clues that confirm their worldview. So, for example, in the Ten Plagues narrative in the book of Exodus, the Bible critics note that the narrative makes frequent mention of Pharaoh's heart as "strong," "hard," "stubborn," or "heavy" (i.e., Pharaoh hardened his heart and wouldn't let the Children of Israel leave Egypt).[1] There are numerous English translations, but the Hebrew text mainly uses two words: *chazak*, which means "strong," and *kaved*, which means "heavy."

The Bible critics assume that each word is a synonym preferred by one of two different authors and accordingly divide the sources between P ("strong") and E ("heavy"). A more inquisitive reader would ask why a single author might be alternating these words.

PHARAOH'S HEART		
SOURCE IN EXODUS	**EXPRESSION**	**ALLEGED AUTHOR**
7:14; 8:11, 28; 9:7, 34; 10:1	*HEAVY*	*E*
7:13, 22; 8:15; 9:12; 14:4, 8, 17	STRONG	P

The Bible uses language precisely. We will withhold extended commentary on the reasons for the author's choice of words. Just a few points will suffice to make clear that "heavy" and "strong" are not synonymous, but the sort of well-chosen variations of meaning that one might expect from a single, skilled author.

In the context of Exodus, a "strong" heart means stubborn. In contrast, "heavy" has a specifically Egyptian meaning,[2] which the Bible's author uses satirically to highlight Pharaoh's wickedness.

In Egyptian mythology, every Egyptian of rank had his own scroll, or "Book of the Dead," to guide him to the afterlife. One of the first major rituals along that underworld journey was "the

Weighing of the Heart." In the process of mummification, the deceased's vital organs were put in a jar. It was believed that his heart would then be placed on a scale in a ceremony supervised by the scribe-god Thoth. The other side of the scale held a feather. If his heart was lighter than a feather, the deceased was considered worthy for the journey and was presented to Osiris, god of the underworld. If his heart was heavy, then he was gobbled up by the monster Ammut, who had the head of a crocodile, the torso of a leopard, and the hindquarters of a hippopotamus, the three most feared animals in proximity.

PAPYRUS OF ANI (C. 1250 BCE, BRITISH MUSEUM NO. 10,470)

An ancient Egyptian papyrus from the era of the Pharaohs depicts an Egyptian official, Ani, going through this process. (He is followed by his wife Thuthu; Egyptians didn't like to die alone, so some had their spouses and servants entombed with them to help with the underworld voyage.) The papyrus shows the jackal-headed god Anubis conducting the weighing, while the ibis-headed scribe-god Thoth (moon god) records the result.

A small baboon, Thoth's assistant, sits on top of the central pillar to see that fair play is done, and a dozen supervisory gods watch from above (very much like our jury system). The jar containing Ani's heart is on the left-hand scale, and on the right is the feather of Ma'at, the goddess symbolic of truth and good order. On the right, the beastly Ammut waits for Ani to fail the test. If Ani succeeds, Thoth declares:

> Hear ye this judgment. The heart of [the one who comes before] Osiris hath in very truth been weighed. . . . It has been found true by trial in the Great Balance. There has not been found any wickedness in him; he has not wasted the offerings in the temples; he has not done harm by his deeds; and he has uttered no evil reports while he was upon earth.

In marked contrast to the above declaration of Thoth, the Bible reports: "But Pharaoh made his heart **heavy** even this time, and he did not send out the people." (Exodus 8:28)

The Bible's author is making a satiric statement about Pharaoh's moral character. Even by the degenerate standards of his own death cult, the author is saying that Pharaoh's heavy heart fails the test.[3]

For all their talk about literary and historical skills and archeological knowledge, the Bible critics overlook the cultural context of the Bible. This oversight reflects an ideological commitment that prefers confirmation of dogma to understanding of the text. A reader of ordinary sophistication, in seeing the constant alternation of two different words, asks *why*. The Bible critics, committed to their hypothesis of multiple authorship, ask *who*.

Snakes, Serpents, and Crocodiles, Oh My

In another example from Exodus, the Bible critics make the same mistake of assuming that the use of two seemingly synonymous words implies two different authors.

In the scene where Moses encounters God at the burning bush, when Moses asks how he will convince the Israelites that he was really sent by God, God tells the prophet to throw down his staff, and the staff becomes a *nachash* (usually translated as "snake"). In the scene in which Moses and Aaron encounter Pharaoh, Aaron throws down his staff and the staff becomes a *tanin* (often translated as "serpent"). The Bible critics therefore assign the former text to E (since E is assumed to be a partisan of Moses), and the latter text to P (since P is assumed to be a partisan of Aaron).

TANIN AND NACHASH				
SOURCE	SYMBOL	OWNER	AUDIENCE	AUTHOR
Burning Bush Episode (Exodus 3)	Staff turns into a *nachash*	Moses' Staff	Israelites	*E*
Sign Before the Plagues Begin (Exodus 7)	Staff turns into a *tanin*	Aaron's Staff	Egyptians	P

Once again, this source division is predicated on the assertion that the priests of Shilo, represented by E, were descendants of Moses, who were playing up their preferred protagonist, while P was a descendant of Aaron, always pushing for his guy to play leading roles. So the Bible critics find synonyms that cluster around these supposed sibling rivals and divide up the text accordingly. However, *nachash* and *tanin* are not synonyms, as a deeper understanding of the text will make clear.

Recall the encounter at the burning bush. God asks Moses to lead his people out of Egypt, and Moses struggles to decline the offer. He voices many objections, one of them being, "But they will not believe me and they will not heed my voice, for they will say, 'Hashem did not appear to you.'" (Exodus 4:1) Allegedly, E is the author of this story.

God offers Moses three signs to show that he is indeed God's messenger. First, he is to cast his staff on the ground, and it becomes a snake. Second, he is to remove his hand from his chest, and it becomes leprous like snow. Third, he is to take water from the Nile, spill it on the ground, turning it into blood.

Ultimately, Moses succeeds in convincing the Israelites that God had sent him. But he and his brother Aaron have no such luck on their first encounter with Pharaoh. Here, in Exodus 7, it is Aaron who throws down his staff before Pharaoh, where it turns into a *tanin*. Then each of Pharaoh's magicians turns his staff into a *tanin*. (Even though Aaron's staff swallows up those of Pharaoh's magicians, Pharaoh remains unmoved.)

So why do we have two different words for the creatures into which Moses' and Aaron's staffs transform? Because they are two different creatures: *nachash* is a snake and *tanin* is none other than the terror of the Nile, the vicious crocodile.

It bears mentioning that in modern Hebrew, *tanin* is the word for crocodile. But this is corroborated in the Bible itself:

"Thus said God, 'Behold, I am against you, Pharaoh, king of Egypt, the great *tanim* [a variant spelling of *tanin*] that crouches within its rivers . . .'" (Ezekiel 29:3)

Apart from the fact that a snake does not crouch nor is its primary habitat Egypt's rivers, as is the case with the crocodile, the author is really making a point of comparing Pharaoh to a *tanin*.

And, indeed, as those who possess training in languages, biblical archeology, and literary and historical skills must surely know, Egyptians worshipped the crocodile as a deity named "Sobek." In the pantheon of Egypt's many gods, Sobek specifically epitomized the might of the Pharaoh and is depicted in hieroglyphics as a man with a crocodile head.

Moreover, the word *tanin* makes its first appearance in the Bible's opening story of creation in Genesis:

"And God created the great *taninim* [plural of *tanin*] and every living being that creeps, with which the waters teemed after their kinds; and all winged fowl of every kind." (Genesis 1:21)

Note that the creation of the *tanin* occurred on the fifth day of creation, along with other sea creatures. Land animals, such as snakes, were created on the sixth day—more evidence that these are two different species. Equally noteworthy is the fact that of all the classes of animal life God created—be it fish, fowl, creeping thing, or beast of the field—the *tanin* is the only species that is specifically identified in the Creation. Just as the snake in the Garden of Eden foreshadowed Moses' presentation of credentials to the Israelites, so too does the earlier appearance of the crocodile help us understand the showdown with Pharaoh in the book of Exodus while making the point that the dreaded crocodile worshipped as a god in Egypt is but a single creation of the one true God.

The Tanin–Crocodile–Pharaoh connection is clear. So what does the Nachash–Snake imagery mean? The staff becoming a snake invokes the memory of the Garden of Eden, which also involved wood (the Tree of Life) and a snake. The snake brought death into the world by counseling Eve to eat the forbidden fruit. So E is using imagery from a J story.

There is now a vivid connection between the three signs given to Moses at the burning bush. They all symbolize God's control over life and death.

MOSES' THREE SIGNS TO THE ISRAELITES (EXODUS 4:1–9)		
Signs at the burning bush assigned to _E_	**Imagery: life & death**	**Parallel source assigned by the Bible critics**
SNAKE *"He cast it on the ground and it became a snake."*	Wood, like the Tree of Life. Snake brought death to the world	**Genesis 2–3—J**
LEPROSY *"And when he took it out, his hand was leprous like snow."*	From living flesh to deathly leprosy	Leviticus—P
BLOOD *"And the water that you take from the Nile will turn to blood."*	Water (life) Blood (death)	First Plague—E, P

Leprosy is also a symbol of death. The white skin coloring is supposed to invoke the image of a corpse, and the ritual for overcoming leprosy in the book of Leviticus is nearly identical to the ritual prescribed for mourners. The intention is to signal that the leper is deserving of death for his behavior (such as slanderous character assassination) and should repent.[4] But P, not E, is the supposed author of the book of Leviticus, which describes this ritual. So, according to the Bible critics, E is using imagery from P (who lived *after* E).

Water is a symbol of life in all of literature, and blood is a pretty straightforward symbol of death. The three signs are part of a unified message: I am the God who controls life and death. I therefore have the power to overcome Pharaoh, the most powerful man in the world. The Bible critics rupture this unity by assigning the story to E, even though the text purposefully echoes themes supposedly written by J and P.

Rather than the two different words indicating two different authors, the variant word choices really indicate two different audiences. To the Israelites, the snake is used as a symbol of God who has the power over life and death. To Pharaoh, who believes in nature-based deities, Aaron's staff becomes the feared crocodile. And although Pharaoh's magicians can do this trick as well, Aaron's staff consumes their staffs.

The Bible's author took the trouble to lay out all of these clues for the curious reader, but the Bible critics did not bother to understand why the author would use different words in different contexts. Because of an intellectually uncurious and unenergetic approach, their students and readers miss out on what is really happening in these stories.

It is easy to say "two different words, two different authors." The challenge is to ask why.

PART III

The Bible's

Unity and Harmony

CHAPTER ELEVEN

Creation, Plagues, and a Talking Donkey: The Bible Critics Make Asses of Themselves

*A highly refined rhetorical device cuts across
the critics' alphabet of authors*

We have seen throughout this book that the Bible critics divide up a text that is united in theme, in metaphor, in style, and in terminology. In the next three chapters, we will demonstrate that the Bible's essential unity goes deeper still. The words we read on the surface are profoundly rooted in a common literary structure evident throughout the Bible. This structure is robust, visible, and clearly evinces the author's meticulous planning and unmistakable literary fingerprints.

We begin "in the beginning."

Genesis begins with a big bang. If set to music, Beethoven's Fifth Symphony, though no match for the Bible's literary power, would be of service. In its first words, the Bible proclaims God's total mastery of the world. God speaks and the world comes into being. He alone creates and puts everything in its place: heavens and earth, seed-bearing trees, sun, moon, and sky, fish and fowl, animals and mankind. The message is that this is God's world and He runs the show:

> In the beginning, Elokim created the heavens and the earth. The earth was astonishingly empty, with darkness upon the surface of the deep, and the Divine Presence hovered upon the surface of the waters. Elokim said, "Let there be light," and there was light. (Genesis 1:1-3)

This revelation was revolutionary. The forces of nature that ancient pagans worshipped appear in chapter 1 of Genesis as mere objects of an all-powerful God. The sun, for example, was widely worshipped as a deity throughout the ancient Middle East. But in Genesis it is the sun that serves God's purpose, somewhat like an electric utility that is at man's command today by the flicking of a switch. Tellingly, the sun is further put in its place in that the word for sun in Hebrew linguistically connotes "servant."[1]

Whereas the Babylonians ascribed power to their sun-god Shamash, the Bible depicts servitude:

> Elokim said, "Let there be luminaries in the firmament of the heaven . . . and they shall serve as signs, and for festivals, and for days and years; and they shall serve as luminaries . . . to shine upon the earth." And it was so. (Genesis 1:14-15)

"And it was so." God speaks and the world obeys. From the opening words to the last verse and everything in between, this theological statement is manifestly the point of chapter 1 of Genesis.

The Triquad

The Bible employs a number of rhetorical devices that serve to unify and amplify its message, giving it recurring rhythms that are contrived so precisely that reading the Bible can be like listening to a song.

We have seen how the Bible's author frequently uses parallelism to make his points. By giving two or more elements a common form, a parallel structure gives the whole a definite pattern, and this pattern is a clue to a deeper meaning. Genesis 1 employs a parallel structure that we will call, for lack of a better term, a "triquad" because of its three–four structure. This pattern, found elsewhere in the Bible, relates three points to each other and then gets to the punch line in the fourth. Take a look at the order of Creation:

ORDER OF CREATION IN GENESIS (P)			
SET	**A. LIGHT**	**B. SEA & AIR**	**C. EARTH**
Set 1	**Day 1** Light	**Day 2** Water and Heaven	**Day 3** Land, Plants, Trees
Set 2	**Day 4** Luminaries	**Day 5** Fish and Birds	**Day 6** Animal, Human, Food
SABBATH			

In the story of Creation, Day 1 matches Day 4 (luminous creations), Day 2 matches Day 5 (extraterrestrial creations), and Day 3 matches Day 6 (earthly creations). After three ascending steps of creation, from physics to botany, come another three ascending steps, from astronomy to physiology, and then comes the punch—the Sabbath—which lies outside of creation and is without parallel.

For added measure, the relative size of the text is also parallel (see below): Day 1 and Day 4 are of medium length; Day 2 and Day 5 are short; and Day 3 and Day 6 are long. This last set of days shares one more commonality: God pronounced all of His creations good, but Day 3 and Day 6 each get two mentions of Divine approval.[2] That is because man and those creations most tied to his maintenance are the climax in God's buildout of the world's infrastructure (Days 1–2–3) and superstructure (Days 4–5–6). Note also that the earlier creations (Days 1–2–3) are stationary, in contrast to the locomotive ability characteristic of the later creations (Days 4–5–6).

THE CREATION			
SET	A	B	C
Set 1	**Day 1** Medium	**Day 2** Small	**Day 3** Large—Twice "Good"
Set 2	**Day 4** Medium	**Day 5** Small	**Day 6** Large—Twice "Good"
SABBATH			

The author P, according to the Bible critics, created a relatively simple yet elegant triquad for the opening of his book.

For greater clarity, and for easier comparison with similar patterns found in the Bible, we transpose the "Order of Creation" chart below.

CREATION (P)		
SET 1		
SUBSECTION	DAY	CREATION
A	1	Light
B	2	Water and Heaven
C	3	Land, Plants, Trees
SET 2		
SUBSECTION	DAY	CREATION
A	4	Luminaries
B	5	Fish and Birds
C	6	Animal, Human, Food
END		
End	7	Shabbat

To really understand the mechanics of biblical parallelism, we need to look at another couple of triquads in play elsewhere in the Bible. Let's look at the story of the Ten Plagues in the book of Exodus.

The Ten Plagues narrative is a masterpiece of parallelism as intricate and refined as a snowflake. No plague was just a punishment. Every aspect of the story is layered in symbolism, and we make no attempt to uncover the full depth of its meaning. We do, however, want to illustrate the triquad structure undergirding the story (see below).[3]

THE TEN PLAGUES (E-P)

SET 1

PLAGUE	MESSAGE	WARNING	LOCATION	TIME	VEHICLE
1st Plague Blood (E-P)	"You will know that I am Hashem." (Exodus 7:17)	Yes	Nile	Morning	Staff
2nd Plague Frogs (E-P)	None	Yes	—	—	Staff
3rd Plague Lice (P)	None	No	—	—	Staff

SET 2

PLAGUE	MESSAGE	WARNING	LOCATION	TIME	VEHICLE
4th Plague Wild Beasts (E)	"You will know that I am Hashem in the midst of the land." (Exodus 8:18)	Yes	Nile	Morning	None
5th Plague Pestilence (E)	None	Yes	—	—	None
6th Plague Boils (P)	None	No	—	—	None

SET 3

PLAGUE	MESSAGE	WARNING	LOCATION	TIME	VEHICLE
7th Plague Hail (E)	"You will know that there is none like Me in all the land." (Exodus 9:14)	Yes	Nile	Morning	Moses' hand/staff
8th Plague Locusts (E)	None	Yes	—	—	Moses' hand/staff
9th Plague Darkness (E)	None	No	—	—	Moses' hands

END

PLAGUE	MESSAGE	WARNING	LOCATION	TIME	VEHICLE
10th Plague Firstborn (E-P)	"And bring a blessing on me too." (Exodus 12:32)	No	—	Midnight	None

Because Pharaoh fails to heed Moses' warning to let his people go so that they may serve God, God inflicts a series of plagues, symbolically beginning at the scene of Egypt's greatest crime, the Nile River, where newborn Hebrew boys were mercilessly cast to their deaths.

Moses strikes the water and it turns into blood, as if uncovering all the blood spilled through Egyptian infanticide. Moses also warns Pharaoh before the plague of the frogs to let his people go, but Pharaoh ignores the warning. Then with no warning comes the plague of lice.

This first set of three plagues establishes a recurring pattern (in Plagues 4–5–6 and 7–8–9). The first plague always comes with a warning, as if to say, "If you don't listen, you're going to get hit." First the warning, then the punishment. Then comes a second warning and a second punishment. Finally Pharaoh asks Moses to stop the plague (of the frogs) and agrees to let Israel go. The plague ends, but Pharaoh fails to live up to his part of the bargain by freeing the Children of Israel; he gets hit a third time with no warning. *Strike three, he's out.*

The pattern is two warnings before Pharaoh gets smacked down. Indeed, it appears that the third plague in each set involves direct body contact, like a disciplinary spank. With cautious avoidance an Egyptian could protect himself from hail, or could keep a broom between himself and a wild beast, but the third plague, lice, was on his skin; the sixth plague, boils, were on his body; and the ninth plague, darkness, was physically and palpably menacing. (Hashem said to Moses, "Stretch forth your hand toward the heavens, and there shall be darkness upon the land of Egypt, and the darkness will be *tangible*.")[4]

After the three sets of three plagues comes the final, fatal blow that is outside of the regular scheme. There are no more warnings and neither will there be any further resistance after so great a punishment. The death of the firstborn of every Egyptian man and beast stands on its own.

Besides punishing the Egyptians in proportion to their treatment of the Hebrew slaves, the tenth plague completes the plague scheme in a way that is parallel to the seventh day's completion of the scheme of creation. Just as God created in six days and rested on the seventh, with the Sabbath a completion and perfection of creation, so, too, was the tenth plague a completion and perfection of Divine retribution.

The Bible's author uses the triquad parallelism of the Ten Plagues to deliver a message, escalating in intensity along with each set of plagues (parallel to the ascending order of creation discussed previously). The message is always delivered to Pharaoh before the first plague in each triplet, always at the same location—the Nile—and always at the same time—the morning. The first message is: "You shall know that I am Hashem." (Exodus 7:17) *I*, and not the Nile, the frogs, nor the earth (when struck, earth's dust became lice): all three were regarded as deities by the Egyptians.

The second message is: "You will know that I am Hashem in the midst of the land" (Exodus 8:18), meaning an immanent God Who is on the scene in Egypt and can make sure His plagues affect only Egyptians and not Israelites.[5]

The third message is: "You shall know that there is none like Me in all the world" (Exodus 9:14), indicating an all-powerful God Who controls the forces of nature, including the heavens that rained down hail, the wind that carried the locust storm, and the symbolic eclipse of the sun that enabled the plague of darkness. These plagues toppled still more Egyptian deities, including the sun-god Ra, one of the chief gods of Egypt.

In sum, the three messages state that there is a God, that He is immanent and in charge—even in Egypt—and that He is most powerful. Then comes the climax in the tenth plague, wherein Pharaoh yields to every one of Moses' conditions, urges Israel to depart with haste, and adds, "And bring a blessing on me, as well!" (Exodus 12:32)

Pharaoh's entreaty goes beyond the theological statements in each of the triplets because it is an admission by Pharaoh of all three. He has learned his lessons. The man who upholds the world's most powerful civilization, in effect the ruler of the world, now acknowledges the true Ruler of the world and asks Moses, a lowly Israelite, to intercede with him for a blessing.

But that's not all. The Bible's author goes even further to strengthen the unity of the text through parallels of time, place, and manner. In a masterful display of literary craft, the author always sets the scene of the first plague of each triplet in the morning; the other six times are unknown, and the tenth plague stands out as taking place at midnight, as befits its dark character. The place where Moses and Pharaoh meet in the first plague of each set is always the Nile; in the second plague of each set the location is presumed to be the palace;[6] in the third of each set there is no meeting (which makes sense because there was no warning).

As we saw in chapter 6, the Bible critics missed all of this. They carved up the ten plagues story between E and P, even going as far as assigning the first two plagues to E and P together, somehow working in tandem across the ages, perhaps with R's assistance. Here is what their individual creative work looks like:

$5\frac{3}{2} + 2\frac{3}{2}$ = 10 PLAGUES	
The Five and Three-Halves Plagues by *E*	**The Two and Three-Halves Plagues by P**
1. *Blood* (half)	1. Blood (half)
2. *Frogs* (half)	2. Frogs (half)
	3. Lice
4. *Wild Beasts*	
5. *Pestilence*	
	6. Boils
7. *Hail*	
8. *Locusts*	
9. *Darkness*	
10. *Firstborn* (half)	10. Firstborn (half)

Not nearly as interesting, is it?

Talking Donkey, Talking Prophet

One more illustration of the triquad, taken from the story of Balaam in the book of Numbers, should help us to determine the author's purpose in using this particular literary form.

The story of Balaam has unique charm in large part because of its talking donkey, a more sympathetic character than the Bible's other talking animal, the cunning snake encountered in Genesis 3. The narrative begins when the Children of Israel encamp at the Plains of Moab, across from their final destination in the Land of Israel. Balak, the king of Moab, is fearful of Israel because of Israel's large numbers and military prowess. Beyond rational fears,

Balak seems to harbor a deep antipathy toward the Israelites, with whom his nation is "disgusted." Rather than negotiate terms of a peaceful passage through Moabite territory, Balak joins forces with the neighboring Midianites and together they seek the good offices of Balaam, a gentile prophet who seems to have a good track record of successfully blessing or cursing people.

A joint Moabite–Midianite delegation bearing gifts asks Balaam to curse Israel in order to make an attack on the hated Israelites succeed. The prophet has the visitors stay the night while he awaits God's instructions. God immediately puts the kibosh on the idea, saying, "You shall not curse the people, for it is blessed." (Numbers 22:12) Balaam therefore sends the delegation back home, but King Balak, determined to curse Israel, keeps sending more and higher-ranking delegates, offering Balaam greater financial inducements to do the job.

Although Balaam points out that no amount in Balak's treasury could make it possible for Balaam to contravene God's word, Balaam nevertheless signals that he would like to take Balak on as a client. He again asks the delegation to spend the night, as if God would change His mind. This time, God takes a different tack. He says that Balaam can go to Moab, but he must say only what God allows him to say.

Balaam should have gotten the clue that this would be a fool's errand, but he rises early to journey to Moab. Blinded by his pursuit of honor and the desire to win the esteem of royalty, Balaam fails to see an angel with his sword drawn standing on the road in front of him. His she-donkey, however, wisely veers off the road. Balaam, in a rush to get to Moab, angrily hits the donkey. This time the angel obstructs the pair's off-road progress. Not only could the donkey not return to the road, but the animal had no choice but to press her master's leg against a nearby wall. Balaam responds with more blows. The angel comes in still closer, leaving the donkey no room to maneuver. It crouches down, and Balaam lets loose his fury on the poor beast.

Then God opens the she-donkey's mouth, where in perfect Hebrew prose the donkey protests, "What have I done to you that you struck me these three times?" (Numbers 22:28) Too angry to notice anything unusual about a donkey talking and without any awareness of the irony of his words, Balaam replies, "Because you mocked me! If only there were a sword in my hand, I would now have killed you!"

The donkey poignantly asks whether she has ever acted in a similarly nonresponsive fashion throughout Balaam's entire lifetime (apparently the donkey and the prophet go way back). Offering no apologies, Balaam answers, "No." He then sees the sword-bearing angel and bows and prostrates himself.

The angel rebukes Balaam for rushing to oppose God's will and says he would have killed Balaam had his donkey not faithfully veered away from the sword three times. Balaam's eyes are now wide open and he wisely offers to return home. But the angel repeats God's message that he go on but speak only the word of God.

The story so far has been a triquad. In three encounters, Balaam is blinded to God's will (as expressed by the angel), but a fourth time he can see (see figure below).

In the concluding portion of the story, Balak and Balaam meet and the king rebukes the prophet for not having come more quickly. This time, however, Balaam—who came close to losing his life for allowing the pursuit of honor to take precedence over obedience to God—has gotten the message, "Behold! Now I have come to you—am I empowered to say anything? Whatever word God puts into my mouth, that shall I speak!" (Numbers 22:38)

Now a second triquad runs parallel to the episode with the angel. Balak takes Balaam up to a mountaintop overlooking the Children of Israel so he can curse them. Instead, Balaam utters

God's blessing. Balak protests and Balaam repeats that he can say only that which God commands him. Balak urges the prophet to pronounce from a different mountaintop, hoping the new scenery will inspire a curse. Again, Balaam blesses, albeit this time with dark implications for his client: "Behold! The people will arise like a lion cub and raise itself like a lion; it will not lie down until it consumes prey, and drinks the blood of the slain." (Numbers 23:24)

Balak tries his "luck" again, "Go now. I shall take you to a different place. Perhaps it will be proper in God's eyes that you will curse them for me from there." (Numbers 23:27)

Balaam's third utterance is no less praiseworthy of Israel and no less menacing to Moab. Balak reacts angrily (Numbers 24:10–11):

> Balak's anger flared against Balaam and he clapped his hands. Balak said to Balaam, "To curse my enemies did I summon you, and behold, you have continually blessed them these three times. Now, flee to your place. I said I would honor you, but—behold—Hashem has withheld you from honor."

After this second set of three is complete comes the punch. Unbidden, Balaam prophesies about the fate of Israel and the fate of Moab "in the end of days." Despite all of Balak's angry pleas and offers of honor, God decrees that Israel is blessed and that Moab is cursed.

The pattern is now clear. Three times Balaam is angry at his donkey for impeding him on his mission to curse Israel. The third time Balaam threatens violence, "If only there were a sword in my hand I would now have killed you!" Then comes the punch: an angel holding a sword almost kills Balaam. Shaken, he now sees the truth: the appearance of the angel reminding him he can only do God's will. The message is that God calls the shots.

Then three times Balak gets angry with Balaam for impeding his mission to curse Israel. The third time his anger is expressed violently (i.e., the clap): "Balak's anger flared against Balaam and he clapped his hands." Then comes the punch: Balaam delivers a fourth blessing, unbidden, and tells Balak that Moab is doomed. Now Balak sees the truth: that neither a prophet for hire nor royal riches determine the destiny of the world. Only God does.[7]

THE BALAAM TRIQUAD (E)		
SET 1	THE DONKEY AND BALAAM	
SUBSECTION	DONKEY	BALAAM
A	Sees the angel	Angry at the donkey
B	Sees the angel	Angry at the donkey
C	Sees the angel	Angry—Wants to kill the donkey
End	Balaam sees the truth (embodied by the angel) that God calls the shots	
SET 2	BALAAM AND BALAK	
SUBSECTION	BALAAM	BALAK
A	Blesses Israel	Angry at Balaam
B	Blesses Israel	Angry at Balaam
C	Blesses Israel	Angry—Wants to hit Balaam
End	Balaam blesses unbidden; Balak sees the truth that God calls the shots	

The Balaam narrative, allegedly written by E, is a masterful display of the author's panache and humor. In the first set of the triquad, Balaam fails to see what his donkey sees. In the second set, Balaam becomes the donkey and Balak becomes Balaam. Now it is Balaam who is frustrated that Balak does not see. This is the Bible's way of making an ass out of Balaam, who was slow to obey God's command.

Conclusion

We have demonstrated three tightly woven narratives employing the same rhetorical device. (As we will see later, this is not the most commonly used rhetorical device.) In each of these disparate stories in three different books of the Bible, it is used when the author wants to make the same point.

In the story of the Creation, God commands the world into existence. The message is God's total mastery of the universe.

In the story of the Ten Plagues, God goes up against the most powerful man in the world. Pharaoh loses and the gods of Egypt prove worthless. God's mastery is so great that He can deploy "smart bombs" that can attack his targets precisely while shielding the population He wishes to protect.

The Balaam narrative is the story of a world-famous prophet who *wants* to curse Israel but who is shown as having no independent power to do so.[8] He ends up being humbled by his own donkey.

So we have three stories, each arrayed in a triquad and each bearing the same message that God is the absolute sovereign of the universe. Now we offer our own triquad: According to the Bible critics, the first story was written by P, the third story was written by E, and the second was co-written by P and E. And the punch: Through their superficial reading of the Bible, the Bible critics miss the point of the story and rip apart the fabric that holds the Bible together. They underestimate its author; hence they overestimate the number of authors.

If the Bible critics are to be believed, then E and P working independently of each other and at different times wrote stories that fit into a remarkably elegant and highly refined rhetorical scheme. There were not actually ten plagues until R inserted P's plagues into E's document in order to match the triquad pattern that P uses in the Creation story and that E uses in the Balaam story.

Isn't it amazing how, by some cosmic coincidence, R was able to cobble these separately written pre-existing documents to make them fit into this complex parallel structure? Imagine two inventors independently designing an abacus, then a third party comes along, merges their designs, and comes up with a supercomputer!

Further confounding matters, though, is that Genesis 1 uses Elokim, while both the stories of the plagues and Balaam use both Elokim and Hashem. So while R deftly replicated the triquad, he displayed no consistent logic in his use of the Divine names.[9]

In earlier chapters, we showed what a mess the Bible critics have made of the Bible, but now we've glimpsed just how orderly it is, indeed, how unified it is. But we have only scratched the surface. In the next chapter, we dig a little deeper to observe a literary structure that is even more pervasive and that, like the triquad, serves as an unmistakable literary fingerprint.

CHAPTER TWELVE

Perfect Parallels:
The Chiasmus

The dominant literary form in the Bible

reveals a startling unity of text

W e saw in the last chapter how the Bible's author uses literary structure to tell a story. We will now show another more prevalent structure. This literary device is called the "chiasmus," so named because it revolves around the center just like the Greek letter *chi* (**X**).

Chiastic Structure

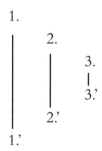

The chiastic structure requires the most extraordinary planning because the first idea is always parallel to the last idea, the second idea is always parallel to the second-to-last idea, the third idea is always parallel to the third-to-last idea, and so on, until you get to the center, which always contains the central point of any given story. We can stipulate that the Bible's author is an intensely organized thinker.

Let's take a very simple example—a single sentence from the book of Genesis:

GENESIS 9:6 (P)

"Whoever sheds the blood of man, by man shall his blood be shed."

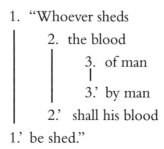

1. "Whoever sheds
    2. the blood
        3. of man
        3.' by man
    2.' shall his blood
1.' be shed."

The central idea of this chiasmus is that the crime of murder must be dealt with through *human* justice (in contrast to religions that would leave such matters to *Divine* justice).

Now that we've taken our first baby step, let's look at a bigger chiasmus from a better-known passage, this one from the book of Exodus:

The Ten Commandments
Exodus 20:2–14—(P)

1. THOUGHT

"I am Hashem your God who took you out of the HOUSE of bondage. . . ."

"You shall have no other gods . . ." (Don't stray after other gods.)

2. SPEECH

"You shall not take the name of Hashem, your God, in vain . . ." (Defaming God and his followers)

(3.) DEED

    A. "Remember the Sabbath day to sanctify it . . ." (Sabbath acknowledges creation and that the earth belongs to God. Israelites are to respect God's property weekly.)

    B. "Honor your father and your mother . . ." (Command regarding family)

        (C.) "Do not murder." (The very centerpiece of the Ten Commandments)

    B.' "Do not commit adultery." (Command regarding family)

    A.' "Do not steal." (Respect the property of others.)

2.' SPEECH

"Do not bear false witness against your fellow." (Defaming other people)

1.' THOUGHT

"Do not covet your fellow's HOUSE."

"Do not covet your fellow's wife . . ." (Do not stray after other women.)

Note the parallels in language between the first two and last two items in the chiasmus. For example, (1) "I am . . . God who took you from the *house* of bondage" mirrors (1'), "Do not covet your fellow's *house*," just as the second element in each of these mirrors the other: (1) "You shall have no other gods" and (1') "Do not covet your fellow's wife." They teach, respectively, that the same God who redeemed Israel from the house of bondage decides the lot of each individual, including what house goes to whom and that idolatry and adultery are alike—one is cheating on God and the other is cheating on your wife.

Also, these first items (1)—about belief in the one God—are in the realm of thought, just as the last two (1')—"Do not covet . . ."—are also in the realm of thought.[1]

The next step in the chiasmus is the commandment (2) about speech (not taking God's name in vain), which is parallel to the ninth commandment (2'), not speaking falsely in a legal proceeding (where one would take an oath in God's name). At the center of the chiasmus are five prohibited deeds (3), signifying that, above all, God is concerned with our actions.

Note, however, that this central part forms a mini-chiasmus of its own. "Remember the Sabbath Day . . ." (A) is related to "Do not steal" (A') because both are testaments to the sanctity of property. The fourth commandment specifically recounts the six days of creation, meaning that the world and everything in it are God's. Just as Israelites are to respect God's property and are to desist from acquiring and manipulating material things one day a week, so, too, is there a commandment to respect the property of others.

Moving along the slope, we come to "Honor your father and your mother . . ." (B), which is parallel to "Do not commit adultery" (B') because both affirm the sanctity of family relationships, parental and spousal. In the very center of our chiasmus (both the mini-chiasmus and the larger one) is "Do not murder" (C), the most immoral action proscribed by the Ten Commandments.

The author seems to be saying that being a moral person involves a high degree of self-control and that immoral thought can lead to immoral speech, which in turn can lead to immoral deeds. The story of Naboth's vineyard (1 Kings 21) is a perfect illustration. King Ahab covets Naboth's property intensely; then his evil queen gets him to talk about what so distresses him; they then scheme to murder Naboth and confiscate his property. Thoughts lead to speech, which leads to a most heinous action.

The totalitarian systems of the twentieth century are good modern-day examples of the state waging war against Judeo–Christian religion based on the Ten Commandments. First the state controlled people's thoughts (Hitler's Youth or Communist indoctrination); then their leaders used speech to vilify their enemies (Jews or capitalists); next they confiscated private property, infiltrated family relationships (by breaking up families or encouraging interfamilial espionage), and ended up murdering on a mass scale.

We've already looked at a single-sentence chiasmus and a chiasmus within a chiasmus comprising a whole story. To further enhance our appreciation for the art of biblical parallelism, let's zoom out a bit to see just how all-encompassing these chiasmi are. Indeed, the entire book of Genesis is made up of them. Below is a mega-chiasmus we call the Genesis Cycle, encompassing the first eleven chapters of Genesis, and coded to get a sense of how J, P, and R all "contributed" to this masterpiece.

The Genesis Cycle

1. **Creation—The Universal Plan** (Genesis 1—(P)—God creates the universe and has high expectations for mankind.)

  2. **Garden of Eden—The Fall of Man** (Genesis 2–3—(J) —Man and Woman eat of the Tree of Knowledge; they become subject to human suffering to remind them of their mortality; they are expelled from Eden.)

   3. **Cain and Abel—Moral Failing** (Genesis 4—(J)— The first siblings fight; Cain murders Abel.)

    4. **Idolatry—Spurning the Ruler of the Earth** (Genesis 4:25—(J)—Idolatry is introduced to the world, and God's name is profaned.)[2]

     (5.) **The Book of Man**—Man's Mortality (Genesis 5—(R)—Ten generations all die in a short period of time; man realizes he is mortal.)

    4.' **Sexual Immorality—Man acts as if He rules the Earth** (Genesis 6—(J)—Man responds to mortality through the use of power and sex.)

   3.' **Flood—Moral Failing—Total Corruption** (Genesis 6–9—A composite of (P) and (J)—Society as a whole is in moral disarray; God brings the Flood.)

  2.' **The Tower of Babel—The Fall of Civilization** (Genesis 11—(J)—Society challenges God, so God fragments a single society into differing and opposing nations, reminding humans that society is never perfect.)

1.' **Abraham—The National Plan** (Genesis 12—(J)—God drops the universal plan [Adam] and picks one individual who will father the chosen nation.)[3]

Genesis begins with the Creation (1), God's universal plan for a world that is good.

Within that world, God established a special place for man. The Garden of Eden (2) represents that ideal existence, where all of our needs were taken care of. But then man, egged on by the snake, has the dubious distinction of being God's first creation to disobey its Creator. This falling out of grace with God explains the harshness of our world, why on an individual level we experience pain and suffering and have to work for a living.

Moving down the slope to the center of the chiasmus is the story of Cain and Abel (3). If in the Garden of Eden story man *falls*, in this story man *fails*. Cain commits a crime of murder and is punished for it by being banished from the presence of God.

Man's estrangement from God spread throughout early civilization, at which time "to call in the Name of Hashem became profaned." (Genesis 4:25) In other words, idolatry was born at this stage of history (4).

Distance from God leads to the center of our chiasmus (5): The chronicles of Man—the ten generations between Adam and Noah—note particularly the age at which people died. Remember, God may have cursed Adam with death, but only during this period does nascent humanity actually see Adam and others dying.

Man reacts to the knowledge of his mortality as people have done throughout history: he seeks eternity through power, glory, and monuments (e.g., the Tower of Babel). So moving away from the center of the chiasmus, we have men acting as though they rule the world, callously taking any women they want (4'). This closely parallels (4) in that the same rare Hebrew verb (*huchal*) is used, which always signals the start of some negative development. At that time people spurned God as Ruler, and now men ("the sons of the rulers") act as if they are in charge, with the strong oppressing the weak.

The struggle for power continues with the generation of Noah (3'), which represents civilization's moral failure and is parallel to the story of Cain and Abel about man's moral failure: "Hashem saw that the wickedness of Man was great upon the earth, and that every product of the thoughts of his heart was but evil always." (Genesis 6:5) This, too, is a story about crime and punishment.

The Tower of Babel story (2') parallels the Garden of Eden story. There is no clear crime, just as in the Garden of Eden. Rather, it is a falling out of grace with God, so to speak. Just as the Garden of Eden story explains why man suffers as an individual, the Tower of Babel story explains why civilization as a whole struggles (e.g., barriers to communication). While these two stories involve a confrontation with God, neither rises to the severity of the middle two stories where man is evil to his fellow man. Adam and Eve act in concert, as do the people of Babel.

We reach the final point of the chiasmus with Abraham (1'), which parallels the Creation. God is not a quitter. His universal plan does not work, so he comes up with a new plan: the national plan. After man repeatedly showed that he would not use his freedom responsibly, God chooses a good man, Abraham, to found a nation. God's purpose is to bring righteousness to the world through Abraham's descendants. The rest of the book of Genesis details the development of that plan.

Now that we've zoomed out for the big picture of Genesis, let's try zooming in on the Garden of Eden story.

Garden of Eden Cycle—(J)

1. There were no thorns and thistles; the creation of man from the dust of the earth (Genesis 2:4–7)

    2. The Garden of Eden is formed for man. (Genesis 2:8–15)

        3. God's command to man forbidding the eating of the Tree of Knowledge (Genesis 2:16–17)

            4. Man names the animals, the formation of the woman (Genesis 2:18–24)

                5. a. "They were both naked (*arumim*) . . ."

                    b. "The man and his wife . . ."

                    © "and they were not ashamed."

                    b.' "Now the snake . . ."

                a.' "Was cunning ( ) . . ." (Genesis 2:25–3:1)

            4.' The snake (animal) corrupts the woman. (Genesis 3:1–5)

        3.' Man violates God's command and eats of the Tree of Knowledge (Genesis 3:6–8)

    2.' God curses mankind; paradise lost (Genesis 3:9–16)

1.' Thorns and thistles will grow from the ground; the eventual return of man to the dust of the earth (Genesis 3:17–21)

    Conclusion: The Expulsion from the Garden of Eden (Genesis 3:22–24)

The author opens this section by stating that no thorns and thistles or grain of the field yet existed when man was created from the dust of the earth (1). God creates an ideal environment for man in the Garden of Eden (2). Except for the fruit of the Tree of Knowledge, He gives man carte blanche to eat whatever he wants (3). Even better, He says it is not good for man to be alone. After Adam rejects the animals as helpmates, God gives him Eve as his partner in life (4). At the center of the chiasmus is the childlike innocence Adam and Eve enjoyed (5).

(In a deft literary touch, the Bible's author tightly brackets the main idea of the story as if to confirm its centrality. The author plays on the Hebrew word *arum*, which is used in two different senses. The first [meaning "naked"] appears three words before "And they were not ashamed," and the second [meaning "cunning"] appears three words after that phrase.[4] In the first instance the man and his wife were blissfully unaware of their nudity; in the second instance the snake cunningly opens Adam's and Eve's eyes to its twisted point of view. This progression represents humanity's loss of innocence: the thematic center of our story. In fact, there are exactly twenty verses before and twenty verses after this midpoint.)

Alas, it all goes south from there as we slope down the chiasmus. Point (4'), about the snake and the woman's temptation, is parallel to (4), which is also about animals and the woman. Point (3'), about the violation of God's command, is parallel to (3), the command that was violated. Then comes (2'), the loss of paradise and curses on mankind, which is parallel to (2), the establishment of paradise for the benefit of mankind. Finally in (1'), Adam is told the land will sprout thorns and thistles, and, even worse, he will eventually return to the earth whence he came, a clear parallel to (1), which states there were not yet thorns and thistles at the time when God created man from the earth.

Then comes a new paragraph (on the actual Hebrew scroll) introducing the Expulsion, and so separated from our chiasmus:

"And having driven out the man, He stationed at the east of the Garden of Eden the Cherubim and the flame of the ever-turning sword, to guard the way to the Tree of Life." (Genesis 3:24)

Aided by the author's design of the chiasmus, the central idea of this story becomes clear. The Garden of Eden was a world of blissful innocence. Our ancestors had a choice: either remain innocent in a trouble-free reality, or become self-conscious ("knowing good and bad") and live a mortal life. Man will always choose to grow up and suffer over living in bliss but remaining a child.

A Built-In Study Guide

Our purpose thus far was to show the mechanics of the chiasmus: We have presented a single-sentence chiasmus (Genesis 9:6); we have presented God's most important revelation (The Ten Commandments); we zoomed out to see the book of Genesis as a whole; and we zoomed in to get a close-up look at the beautiful Garden of Eden. We didn't bother noting that J and P are said to have sketched out, at different times, the plan for the book of Genesis; we will get to that next.

For now it bears mentioning that in taking the trouble to structure these stories so precisely, it is as though the author included a built-in study guide to help readers understand his work. One can readily see that the Ten Commandments are not a randomly selected group of laws. They communicate the author's insight that a moral person must guard his thoughts, lest they lead to immoral speech, and guard his tongue, lest it bring about immoral behavior. And one can see more clearly what the issues were in man's fall in the Garden of Eden, including the author's explanation as to how grain became the staple of our diet. It was a form of punishment. Rather than pluck fruit from a tree, man was supposed to struggle through thorns and thistles for his daily bread.

Seeing the exceptional literary skill and meticulous planning that went into the creation of the Bible's stories, one can better appreciate the folly of the Bible critics' arguments. One of their more sophisticated examples of multiple authorship is the story of Noah. The Bible critics pull apart strands of that lengthy story and endeavor to show that it is really two interwoven stories that can be read separately. But it turns out there really *is* a unified plan behind this story, which takes the form of this rather large chiasmus:[5]

The Flood (P-J)

1. The downfall of mankind, sexual sin, Noah found favor in Hashem's eyes (6:18)—(J)

2. The story of Noah, his sons: Shem, Ham, and Japheth (6:9–11)—(P)

3. God commands Noah to build the ark (6:12–16)—(P)

4. God announces the coming of the flood (6:17)—(P)

5. Covenant with Noah (6:18) —(P)

6. The command regarding the animals (6:19–20)—(P)

7. Food in the ark (6:21–22)—(P)

8. Command to enter the ark and bring seven clean animals (7:1–3)—(J)

9. Seven days waiting for the flood (7:4–5)—(J); Noah's age (7:6)—(P); Noah realizes that the flood begins (7:7)—(J); The animals enter the ark (7:8–9)—(P)

10. Seven days waiting for the flood (7:10)—(P)

11. Summary of all who enter the ark (7:11–15–16a)—(P)

12. Hashem shuts Noah in (7:16b)—(J)

13. Forty days of flood (7:17a)—(J)

14. Waters increase, lifting the ark, mountains are covered with water, all life perishes (7:17b–23) —(J & P)

15. One hundred fifty days, waters prevail (7:24)—(P)

16. God remembers Noah—(P) The flood ends (8:1–2)— (P & J)

15.' One hundred fifty days waters abate (8:3)—(J & P)

14.' Mountaintops become visible as the waters abate (8:4–5)—(P)

13.' Forty days of waiting (8:6a)—(J)

12.' Noah opens the ark's window (8:6b)—(J)

11.' Raven and dove leave ark (8:7–9)—(P & J)

10.' Seven days waiting for the waters to subside (8:10–11)—(J)

9.' Seven more days waiting for the waters to subside; the dove leaves and does not return (8:12)—(J); Noah's age (8:13a)— (P); Noah realizes that the earth is visible (8:13b)—(J); The effects of the flood are gone (8:14)—(P)

8.' Command to leave the ark (8:15–19)—(P); Sacrifice of clean animals (8:20–22)—(J)

7.' Food outside the ark (9:1–4)—(P)

6.' Relationship of man and animals (9:5–7)—(P)

5.' Covenant with all flesh (9:8–10)—(P)

4.' No flood in the future, the rainbow (9:11–17)—(P)

3.' Farewell to the ark (9:18)—(J)

2.' Shem, Ham, and Japheth (9:19)—(J)

1.' Downfall of Noah; sexual sin; Shem is favored by Noah (9:20–27)—(J)

The Bible critics were not aware how frequently J completes P's thoughts (or vice versa). They would probably do well simply to give this chiasmus to either J *or* P. But how do you choose? Looking at the previous chiasmi in this chapter, you can see that some are assigned to J and some to P (and some to both J and P). Whom should the Bible critics designate as their chiasmus expert?

Complicating matters, it turns out that E also knows how to plot his story in a chiasmus:

Amalek (Exodus 17:8–16—E)

1. **Amalek wages war against Israel**
   "Amalek came and battled Israel in Rephidim."

 2. **Preparation for war**
    "Moses said to Joshua: 'Choose people for us and go do battle with Amalek; tomorrow I will stand on top of the hill with the staff of God in my hand.'"

  3. **Physical war**
     "Joshua did as Moses said to him, to do battle with Amalek."

   4. **Spiritual war**
      "And Moses, Aaron, and Hur ascended to the top of the hill."

    ⑤ **THE SECRET TO JEWISH VICTORY**
       "It happened that when Moses raised his hand Israel was stronger,
       And when he lowered his hand Amalek was stronger."

   4.' **Spiritual war**
      "Moses' hands grew heavy, so they took a stone and put it under him and he sat on it, and Aaron and Hur supported his hands, one on this side and one on that side, and his hands remained steady until the sun set."

  3.' **Physical victory**
     "Joshua weakened Amalek and its people with the sword's blade."

 2.' **Aftermath**
    "Hashem said to Moses: 'Write this as a remembrance in the Book and recite it in the ears of Joshua, that I shall surely erase the memory of Amalek from under the heavens.' Moses built an altar and called its name "Hashem is My Miracle"; and he said: 'For the hand is on the throne of God . . .'"

1.' **God's war against Amalek**
   "Hashem maintains a war against Amalek, from generation to generation."

Complicating matters further still, it turns out the Bible critics can't even call E their Amalek expert since D also composed a chiasmus about Israel's eternal enemy:

Amalek (Deuteronomy 25:17–19—D)

1. Recollection
"Remember . . ."

> **2. What Amalek did to you**
> "What Amalek did to you . . ."
>
> > **3. Difficult times**
> > "On the way, when you were leaving Egypt, that he happened upon you on the way, and he struck those of you who were hindmost, all the weaklings at your rear, when you were faint and exhausted, and he did not fear God."
> >
> > **3.' Good times**
> > "It shall be that when Hashem, your God, gives you rest your God, gives you as an inheritance to possess it . . ."
>
> **2.' What you should do to Amalek**
> "You shall wipe out the memory of Amalek from under the heaven . . ."

1.' Recollection
"You shall not forget!"

So we see that J, E, P, and D each knew how to write his own chiasmus. Maybe that's just what ancient Near East writers did. But how did three of them living at different times get to be in on the same planning meeting?

Abraham Cycle (J-*E*-P Other)

1. Abraham's first test: Abraham sacrifices his past, Divine revelation, and blessing—*Lech lecha* (12:1–6)—(J)

  2. Abraham calls out in God's name in Canaan (12:7–8)—(J)

    3. Taking of Sarah in Egypt, separation from Lot (12:8; 13)—(J)

      4. Destruction of Sodom, Lot's downfall, and Abraham's rescue of Lot (14)—(Other)

        5. Promise of Land; Abraham described as Tzaddik (Righteous) (15)—(J)

          6. Sarah's struggle with Hagar, the blessing of Ishmael (16)—(J)

            (7.) THE COVENANT OF CIRCUMCISION—A PROMISE OF NATIONHOOD. ABRAHAM AND SARAH GET NEW NAMES (17)—(P)

          6.' Sarah's reward, the blessing of Ishmael (17)—(P)

        5.' Promise of a child and its justification: Abraham is the only Tzaddik (Righteous) (18)—(J)

      4.' Destruction of Sodom, Abraham's rescue of Lot, and Lot's downfall (18–19)—(J-P)

    3.' Taking of Sarah in Gerar (E), Isaac's birth (P), separation from Ishmael (E) (20–21)—(E-P)

  2.' Abraham calls out in God's Name in the Land of the Philistines (21)—(J)

1.' Abraham's final test: Abraham sacrifices his future, Divine revelation, and blessing—*Lech lecha* (22)—(E)

Recall that the cycle of stories in Genesis begins with God's universal plan for the world. When that plan fails because of man's sin, God initiates a new national plan based on the seed of the righteous Abraham, progenitor of a new nation. This national plan unfolds throughout the balance of Genesis through four sub-cycles, each a beautifully complex chiasmus.

The Abraham cycle opens with the patriarch's first test (1): he is forced to sacrifice his past in order to fulfill his destiny as the father of the nation of Israel. The chiasmus closes with Abraham's final test (1'): he is asked to sacrifice his future (his son Isaac) to prove once and for all his fitness for God's national plan. The verse that introduces his first test (Genesis 12:1) begins with the words,

Lech lecha, a semantically unusual way of saying, "Go." The verse that introduces Abraham's final test (Genesis 22:2) also includes that highly unusual word combination, *Lech lecha*.

We have the same linguistic bracketing in steps (2) and (2') of the chiasmus. First Abraham "calls out in God's name" as he sojourns in the land of Canaan; at the end of our story he "calls out in God's name" as he sojourns in the land of the Philistines. In each case, the author works in the same unusual phrasing.

Finally, within this exquisite literary frame, we find the central message (7) of this story: that God will establish an everlasting covenant specifically through Isaac, the offspring of Abraham and Sarah. (Genesis 17:16–21)

Yet despite all that the author does to fine-tune this poetic symmetry, the Bible critics say that J wrote the first part of this story, P wrote its central idea, and E closed the chiasmus. Taking a close look at the Abraham Cycle, does it make sense that three authors working independently of one another could have written this? That would be like taking a shuffled deck of cards, throwing it up in the air, and watching the cards fall into perfect numerical order.

At this point, we trust our readers are comfortable with the way the chiasmus works. We therefore provide the balance of the book of Genesis through its remaining chiasmi, without adding any further narration. Then, in the next chapter, we will show yet another surprising device, beyond the triquad and the chiasmus, that illustrates the order and unity that a single creator alone could provide.

Isaac Cycle (J)

1. Jacob supplants his brother Esau, taking his birthright (25)
   - (2) THE STORY OF ISAAC (26)
1.' Jacob supplants his brother Esau, taking his blessing (27)

Jacob Cycle (J-*E*-P-R̶)[6]

1. Introduction: "And this is the history of Isaac, son of Abraham: Abraham begot Isaac. (R) Isaac was forty years old when he took Rebecca . . . as a wife for himself." (P) (25:19–20)

   2. Rebecca's difficult pregnancy, birth of Jacob, Esau loses his birthright (J) (25:19–34)

      3. Strife, deception, and covenant with a foreigner (Isaac versus Abimelech) (J) (26)

         4. Jacob deceives Esau, steals his blessing, Jacob fears Esau's retribution (J), Jacob flees from Canaan (P) (27:1–28:9)

            5. Jacob's departure from Canaan, Jacob sees angels. (E) (28:11–12)

               6. Jacob escapes to his uncle Laban. (J) (29:1–14)

                  7. Jacob labors for his wives. (J) (29:15–30)

                     ⑧ THE BIRTH OF THE CHILDREN OF ISRAEL (E–J) (29:31–30:24)

                       A. Birth of four children to Leah (J) (29: 31–35)

                         B. Story: Rachel's frustration at being barren (E) (30: 1–2)

                           C. Birth of two children to Rachel's maid (E) (30:3–8)

                           C.' Birth of two children to Leah's maid (E) (30:9–13)

                       B.' Story: Rachel schemes to end her barrenness. (E) (30:14–16)

                     A.' Birth of four children to Leah and Rachel (E) (30:17–24)

                  7.' Jacob labors for money. (J) (30:25–42)

               6.' Jacob escapes from his uncle Laban. (E) (30:43–31:55)

            5.' Jacob's return to Canaan, Jacob meets angels (E) (32:1–2)

         4.' Jacob prepares to meet his brother Esau, prepares a deception (gift), fears Esau, earns the blessing from an angel, reconciles with Esau, and returns to Canaan. (E) (32–33)

      3.' Strife, deception, and covenant with a foreigner (Jacob versus Shechem) (J) (34)

   2.' Jacob receives the blessing (P) (35:9–15), Rachel dies at childbirth (E) (35:16–20), Reuben loses birthright (J) (35:21–22), the twelve tribes are established. (P) (35:22–26)

1.' End: "Jacob came to Isaac his father, at Mamre . . . Isaac's days were one hundred eighty years. And Isaac expired and died . . . his sons, Esau and Jacob, buried him." (P) (35:27–29)

Who Really Wrote The Bible?

The Children of Israel Cycle (J-E-P-R)

1. The rift in Jacob's family: the family is together in Canaan; Joseph is seventeen years old; the reasons for the rift: (a) Joseph lacks humility, has dreams of superiority and rulership over his brothers, (b) the brothers are jealous and hate Joseph, the brothers attack Joseph and attempt to kill him, Jacob mourns Joseph. (Genesis 37)—(J E P R)

2. Judah the leader: Judah repents, earning his role as his brothers' future leader, gives birth to twins who compete, the younger one becoming the forefather of a future Jewish leader. (Genesis 38)—(J)

3. Joseph learns and proves his humility through trials and tribulations in Egypt before he becomes the King's viceroy; these are presented in three episodes:

   a. Bad: 1st Descent, Joseph is sold into slavery. (Genesis 39)—(J)

   b. Bad: 2nd Descent, Joseph is thrown in jail. (Genesis 39)—(J)

   c. Good: Joseph is summoned by Pharaoh and humbly interprets Pharaoh's dreams. (Genesis 40–41)—(E)

   Conclusion: Joseph is estranged from his family, forced to settle in Egypt, adopts an Egyptian name, marries an Egyptian woman, and has two sons. (Genesis 41)—(E)

3.' The brothers learn and prove their repentance through trials and tribulations in their several descents to Egypt; before Joseph reveals his identity to them, they are presented in three episodes:

   a. Bad: 1st Descent, Joseph does not reveal his identity (Genesis 42)—(J); Joseph jails Simon. (Genesis 42)—(E)

   b. Bad: 2nd Descent, Joseph does not reveal his identity and threatens to jail Benjamin. (Genesis 43–44)—(J)

   c. Good: Judah steps up and proves the brothers' repentance by offering himself instead of Benjamin. (Genesis 44–45)—(J)

   Conclusion: Joseph is united with his family, arranges for his father to settle in Egypt (Genesis 45—J); census of Jacob's family—list of their names (Genesis 46—P); Joseph sows the seeds of the future and the separate Israelite society within Egypt. (Genesis 47—J, P)

2.' Joseph the ruler: Joseph's administration of Egypt (Genesis 47—E); Jacob's adoption of Joseph's two sons (Genesis 48—P) who compete, the younger one becoming the father of a future Israelite leader. (Genesis 48—E)

1.' Reconciliation in Jacob's family: Jacob lives out his last seventeen years in Egypt; Jacob assigns roles to his twelve children; honoring Judah and Joseph; Jacob dies and is mourned by Joseph (Genesis 49–50—J); the brothers are worried about Joseph, but Joseph comforts them with words of peace. (Genesis 50—E)

- 154 -

CHAPTER THIRTEEN

The Bible's Secret Code

*Keyword patterns point to meaning of text
and evidence of author*

The Bible does not merely tell charming tales. As we have seen, the Bible arrays its stories in such a way as to subtly direct the development of the story, organizing and furthering the plot, and communicating deeper moral lessons. Indeed, in every instance, literary structure is tied to meaning.

In that regard, we believe the author of the Bible left hints, a Bible code, if you will, of the author's purpose in each and every part of the Bible.

Before we introduce the code, we must make clear that we do not endorse any of the so-called Bible codes that have been popularized in recent decades. Neither the Torah nor the Hebrew Bible in its entirety shies away from making predictions about the future in clear and testable terms. It would not fit the author's character to resort to cryptic clues to foretell the terrorist plot of 9/11, for example, à la Nostradamus.

The real Bible code does not involve pseudo-scientists using sophisticated computer programs to make predictions about the future. Rather, it offers a user-friendly guide that any layman can use to enhance his understanding of the Bible. The code, simply, is seven.

Anyone with even passing acquaintance with Judaism has some notion that the number seven is highly symbolic in the Bible. There are seven days of creation (told in seven paragraphs); the Sabbath recurs every seven days; there are seven days of Passover and the Festival of Tabernacles (Sukkot); there are seven weeks between Passover and the Festival of Weeks (Shavuot); the menorah has seven branches; there are seven species of vegetation and fruit native to the land of Israel; there is a sabbatical (seventh) year and a jubilee year (which follows seven cycles of seven years). If a Jew were asked to name the digit that comes up most often in Judaism—no contest—he or she would pick seven.

So it is no surprise that this numerical preference is evidenced in the Bible text itself in what we call the Code of Seven. To learn more about what the author is trying to say, all one need do is look at which words appear seven times or a multiple of seven times. It is really that simple (for the reader—but imagine how difficult it would be for a writer to code his book this way).

Let's see if the Code of Seven can aid our search for meaning in the Bible. We'll begin in the beginning:

The figure below shows the Hebrew words that occur in multiples of seven in chapter 1 of Genesis. Note that in the Hebrew language, articles and prepositions are added to the nouns they introduce, so in the first example, "earth" (*eretz*), we also include "the earth" (*ha'aretz*) and "on the earth" (*ba'aretz*).

GENESIS 1—P
35—אלקים—Elokim
21—ארץ—Earth

14—מים—Water

7—טוב—Good

7—ויהי כן—And It Was So

The Code of Seven yields the following keywords: "Elokim" (35 times); "earth" (21 times); "water" (14 times); "good" (7 times); "and it was so" (7 times).[1]

As you can see, chapter 1 of Genesis is mainly about God (who gets the most mentions). But if you string together all of these recurring keywords, what you find is a perfect summary of the theme of the story:

Elokim manipulated the earth and water, God's creations were good, and they obeyed ("and it was so") everything God said.

The message of chapter 1 of Genesis—ascertainable by a simple reading of the text, aided by its underlying triquad literary structure, and reinforced by the Code of Seven—is simply that God is Master of the universe.

Let's now look at the Code of Seven as a shortcut aid in understanding the "second account" of creation in Genesis 2–3.

Here are its keywords: "man" and "woman" (21 times); "tree" (14 times); "good" (7 times); "soil" (7 times); and "field" (7 times).

Whereas the first account of creation was largely about God, these keywords indicate that the second story in Genesis is primarily about *man* and *woman* and how the food they were given to eat from *trees* were among the many *good* things God created until—because of man's sin—the *soil* was cursed, forcing man to work the *field*.

(Hence this story is not at all concerned with the Creation as the Bible critics claim, and why should it be? Everything was already created in chapter 1 of Genesis. Genesis 2–3 is a separate and not at all redundant story, whose main concern is man's relationship with God.)

GENESIS 2–3—J

21—איש-אשה—Man, Woman

14—עץ—Tree

7—טוב—Good

7—אדמה—Soil

7—שדה—Field

A cornerstone of the documentary hypothesis is that there are two redundant creation stories written by two different authors (P and J) using different names of God. And yet both coded their stories in exactly the same way, expressing their key ideas in sevens.

We saw in the incredibly intricate, highly planned story of Balaam that it shared the same underlying triquad as the Creation story in Genesis 1, even though Balaam was supposed to have been written by E, and the Creation story by P. Well, once again, E and P were on the same page, this time with respect to the Code of Seven.

As you might guess, the keywords are "curse" (7 times); "honor" (7 times); "donkey" (14 times); and "bless" (14 times). Balaam was trying to *curse* Israel so he could be *honored* by the Moabite king. But Balaam ends up being humbled by his *donkey* and forced to *bless* Israel.

So if the Bible critics are to be believed, two distinct authors (P and E) separated by time, place, and ideology not only pull off a triquad independently but also manage to use the same seven-code!

NUMBERS 22–23–24—E

7—ארור—Curse

7—כבד—Honor

14—אתון—Donkey

14—ברך—Bless

Not surprisingly, D, too, knows the code:

"For Hashem, your God, is bringing you to a good **Land**—
a **Land** with streams of water, of springs and underground
water coming forth in valley and mountain; a **Land** of
wheat, barley, grape, fig, and pomegranate; a **Land** of oil-
olives and date-honey; a **Land** where you will eat bread
without poverty—you will lack nothing there; a **Land**
whose stones are iron, and from whose mountains you
will mine copper. You will eat and you will be satisfied,
and bless Hashem, your God, for the good **Land** that He
gave you." (Deuteronomy 8:7–10)

This passage stresses that God is bringing the Children of Israel
to a good land that will provide for their material and spiritual
sustenance. There is also a subtler seven in this same passage. Can
you find it?

It is the seven species of food native to the Land of Israel:
wheat, barley, grapes, figs, pomegranates, olives, and dates. Could
you think of a more eloquent way to express an attachment to the
land than its natural bounty?

So here we have four stories, supposedly written by P, J, E, and
D. Each consistently expresses its main ideas in multiples of seven.
And, once again, the Bible critics awkwardly divide up the Bible
because they did not examine the Bible carefully enough to see
the unifying seven code embedded throughout.

Study Guide Par Excellence

The examples above (except for D's) were already familiar from
earlier chapters of the book. But these are in no way a specially
selected few. In fact, the Code of Seven can be found throughout
the Bible, and, like the center of the chiasmus, it often guides us to

the main idea of that passage. Let's take a look at a few more stories the Bible critics assign to J.

We begin with a short, single-seven story: the story of Cain and Abel. What one word comes to mind in this story? (Hint: What's the central question that this story asks?)

You probably came up with the word "brother." No one needs a rabbi, a teacher, or a scholar to tell him that the central question that readers are supposed to grapple with is Cain's retort to God, "Am I my brother's keeper?" Much of the rest of the Bible is a ringing affirmative response to this question. In fact, its first book, Genesis, is consumed with the question of how brothers should relate to each other, and it concludes only when Judah demonstrates that he *is* his brother's (Benjamin's) keeper (after he and his other brothers had already betrayed Joseph).

So it is little surprise that the keyword appearing seven times in this story (Genesis 4:1–15) is brother.

GENESIS 4—J

7—אח—Brother

As the story of Genesis moves along, we get a picture of humanity as a pretty sorry lot. Adam and Eve failed; Cain killed Abel; Noah was worthy of being saved but not of perpetuating God's will in the world. When we get to Abraham, God's faith in humanity, as it were, is restored. Abraham is a man of God. He is willing to subordinate his own will and wisdom to follow difficult Divine instructions; for example, God asks him at the age of seventy-five to take his wife and to leave their home and parents and move to a new land. Upon his arrival in this new land, there is a drought and Abraham must immediately move to another land, Egypt, in order to survive.

Much more can be said about these crucial chapters, but, as

always, the Code of Seven summarizes it well. The focus is on **Abraham** (then called Abram), a special man who has devoted himself to the value system that **Hashem** desires in people. A key characteristic that distinguishes him from other men with potential (e.g., Adam, Noah) is that he has a partner—*his wife*—who fully shares this value system, based on their faith in **Hashem**. Abraham and Sarah withstand the trials of first moving to a new land (Canaan) and then moving again to *Egypt*, where Sarah is kidnapped. The family manages to leave Egypt with great wealth, but their wealth causes the first fissure in this unified group of ethical monotheists. Abraham's nephew Lot goes his own way to the plain of the Jordan (Sodom), because it is in his eyes "like the land of Egypt." They all left Egypt, but Egypt did not leave all of them. Not for the last time in history, material gains bring about an erosion of spiritual values.

GENESIS 12–13—J
14—אברם—Abram

7—אשת—His Wife

7—י-ה-ו-ה—Hashem

7—מצרים—Egypt

Chapters 18 and 19 of Genesis follow up on Lot, whom we last saw moving to Sodom in the plain of the Jordan. Sodom is an evil city, whose people's horrific treatment of strangers calls out for Divine judgment and destruction. Abraham, upon hearing of God's plan, famously negotiates with God about saving the city of Sodom. "Abraham came forward and said, 'Will you also stamp out the righteous along with the wicked?'" (Genesis 18:23)

Abraham suggests that if fifty righteous people could be found in Sodom, God should spare the city. God informs Abraham that there are not fifty righteous people there. So Abraham asks if there are forty-five such people, forty, and so forth. God and Abraham end up agreeing that if God could find just ten righteous people, He would save Sodom.

GENESIS 18–19—J

7—מצא—Find

7—צדיק—Righteous

7—סדם—Sodom

Genesis 34 tells the story of the rape of Dinah. Having moved from the countryside of Haran to the city of Shechem, Dinah, the daughter of Jacob and Leah, goes out to see the "daughters of the land." The prince himself, also named Shechem, "saw her, he took her, lay with her, and violated her." Only after the fact do he and his father try to offer terms of marriage to Dinah's father.

Two keywords cause us to focus on the relationship between *daughter* and *city*, and indeed the link seems fairly obvious as the story unfolds. The safety of one's daughter is no greater than the community standards of the city in which one lives. The author seems to underscore this point explicitly at the story's conclusion when Dinah's brothers take revenge on the people of the city (who are portrayed as at least acquiescing to Shechem's ploys at town hall meetings at the city gate).

"The sons of Jacob . . . plundered the city which had defiled their sister." (Genesis 34:27) It is as though the city had defiled Dinah. As the saying goes, "it takes a village to raise a child"; apparently it takes a village to rape a child. Were it not for the evil tolerated by the people of the city of Shechem, Jacob's daughter would be free to visit the daughters of the land.

GENESIS 34—J

7—בת—Daughter

7—עיר—City

Genesis is peppered with sevens, but E appears to be as fluent with them as J. Genesis 21 is about the birth of Isaac, ensuring the continuation of Abraham's seed, and the alliance between Abraham and Abimelech. The keywords in these stories are *Abraham* and *Abimelech*, each mentioned seven times. What's the connection? This relationship will benefit *Abraham's* successor in later times when the people of *Abimelech's* land are hostile to Isaac, who nevertheless gains protection through his own treaty with *Abimelech*.

GENESIS 21—E

7—אברהם—Abraham

7—אבימלך—Abimelech

Genesis 41 sets the scene of Israel's sojourn in Egypt. The four keywords tell the story:

Egypt avoids *hunger* when Joseph *solves* Pharaoh's *dream*.

GENESIS 41—E

14—מצרים—Egypt

7—רעב—Hunger

7—פטר—Solve

7—חלום—Dream

In Exodus 17, the evil nation of Amalek attacks Israel. God performs a miracle: as long as Moses, positioned on top of a hill, keeps his hands raised, Israel prevails over Amalek; when his hands tire, Amalek wins. The procedure teaches Israel to look heavenward for its military success. A series of three sevens tells the story: *Moses'* raised *hands* prevail over *Amalek*.

EXODUS 17—E

7—משה—Moses

7—יד—Hand

7—עמלק—Amalek

In Exodus 18, the keywords are *Jethro* (seven times) and *father-in-law of Moses* (seven times) because the passage is a study in Jethro's personal growth and his deepening connection to the people and the God of Israel. Jethro is first described both as the "priest of Midian" and "the father-in-law of Moses," but subsequently only as the father-in-law of Moses. Despite his former high status as a priest, he finds even greater distinction in being a relation by marriage to the man who led the Children of Israel out of Egypt. This former priest of Midian even blesses the God of Israel and offers advice on organizing the nation's judicial system.

EXODUS 18—E

7—יתרו—Jethro

7—חתן משה—Father-In-Law of Moses

Numbers 12 is about God's punishment of Miriam for her criticism of Moses. It's a study of Miriam and the strict judgment applied to a prophetess of her standing. Fittingly, the keyword appearing seven times is *Miriam*, who instigated this episode.

NUMBERS 12—E

7—מרים—Miriam

Like his colleagues J and E, P apparently was also a prolific practitioner of the Code of Seven. Genesis 9, about God's post-diluvian covenant, is a straightforward example. After a flood that destroys all life except for Noah, his family, and the animals in their care, God makes a pact with all flesh that He will never again allow all the living to perish. The word *covenant*, woven through the text seven times, ties down this message.

GENESIS 9—P

7—ברית—Covenant

We learn about another covenant in Genesis 17. This one is between God and Abraham and the offspring that Abraham will have through his wife Sarah. And so the keyword is *seed* (as in "offspring"), appearing seven times, focusing reader attention on God's promise to develop a great nation as his agent in history. Humanity has been a failure up until now, hence the Flood. With Abraham, however, God finds the kind of character he was looking for to intergenerationally promulgate a set of values—the original "family values," if you will.

GENESIS 17—P

7—זרע—Seed

The book of Leviticus opens with instructions on how the Children of Israel are to express ritualistically their closeness to God. Remember, their experience at Sinai was marred by the sin of the Golden Calf, but the reconciliation of God and His people was solidified in the building of a Tabernacle where God could dwell with them. Leviticus therefore offers instruction in the different kinds of voluntary offerings, and these instructions are punctuated seven times with the phrase, *a fire offering, a satisfying aroma to Hashem.*[2]

The fact that this term is repeated seven times serves as a clue as to what is most important in these opening instructions. The point seems to be that God is open to a relationship with individual members of the Children of Israel, which is consecrated through these ritual acts. God "consumes," as it were, these fire offerings, and the act of bringing them—of coming close to God—pleases Him. The moral of the story is more significant than many readers, who view Leviticus as a monotonous guide to priestly practices, suspect. It is about nothing less than the individual's ability to maintain a relationship with God through sincere, voluntary acts.

LEVITICUS 1–2–3—P

אשה ריח ניחוח לי-ה-ו-ה —7—A Fire Offering, A Satisfying Aroma to Hashem

The next two chapters of Leviticus change the topic from voluntary offerings to mandatory ones. While the former offerings are celebratory and used to build a relationship with God, the latter are given as sin offerings and serve to repair relations strained because of careless error. The sin offering is thus no different than a husband and wife making the word "sorry" a regular part of their vocabulary in order to move on after hurting one another through inadvertent actions.

Readers who are not paying close attention to Leviticus 4–5 might wrongly assume that the "sin" and "guilt" offering rituals atone for the intentional sins of the Children of Israel. In fact, there is no ritual for intentional sins; individuals must repent and change their behavior. To help attentive readers get the point, P codes these chapters with the keyword *unintentional*.

LEVITICUS 4–5—P

7—שגג—Unintentional

By chapters 6 and 7 of Leviticus, many a reader glazes over at the seeming repetition: more on elevation offerings, meal offerings, sin offerings, guilt offerings, and peace offerings. That is why, once again, we must marvel at the Code of Seven, which clarifies what the author is trying to communicate to the reader. The keyword appearing seven times in these two chapters is *Torah*, in its narrow sense meaning "procedure." Each category of offering is introduced by words to the effect of "this is the procedure for" (the elevation offering, meal offering, etc.).

With help from the Code of Seven, we can now readily see that the first five chapters of Leviticus tell individuals what offerings to bring in different scenarios; the next two chapters address a different audience—the priests ("Command Aaron and his sons . . .")—and detail the specific procedures for performing the offering. Once again, the Code of Seven comes to the rescue of readers too quick to succumb to the sense of déjà vu that has turned off many readers of Leviticus.[3]

LEVITICUS 6–7—P

7—תורה—Procedure

The book of Numbers can also be decoded with the author's keyword system. Chapter 19, for example, is about the mysterious ritual of the red cow. Contact with a dead human being is considered the ultimate level of impurity, and the ashes of the red cow are the ultimate cure. Not surprisingly, the keyword occurring seven times is *pure*.

NUMBERS 19—P

7—טהור—Pure

We have seen that the texts attributed to J, E, and P each have numerous seven codes to their credit. We also showed a single-seven D example (involving the word "land") in the introduction to this chapter. Now we'll show that even D is capable of fancier literary flourishes involving two Code of Seven keywords.

After warning about the curses that will befall Israel for breaking faith with God, Deuteronomy 30 reminds Israel of the blessings that await them for returning to God. The message is obvious. God is the source of curses and the source of blessings. Israel's fate does not depend on happenstance but on *God*, who desires their *return*.

DEUTERONOMY 30—D

14—ה-ו-ה-י—God

7—שב—Return

So according to the Bible critics, J, E, P, and D, all share a predilection for sevens and have the literary talent to code their text this way. But wait—there's more. Even R—in the skimpy bits of infill that he is credited with—manages to use the Code of Seven.

Numbers 9:15–23 relates that all the Children of Israel's travels through the wilderness were *according to the word of Hashem*. When they broke camp and journeyed, it was *according to the word of Hashem*, and when they stopped and set up a new camp, it was *according to the word of Hashem*.

Why not just have one topic sentence stating this concept rather than repeating the phrase seven times? The author seems to be stressing the obedience of the Children of Israel and their absolute reliance on God.[4] If God's cloud lifted inconveniently at night, after only one day of encampment, the Children of Israel obediently followed, and if the cloud lingered in the same place for an entire year, they did not restlessly journey on their own initiative. This was a great merit of the Children of Israel, noted in a book (Numbers) that is particularly frank about their many failings.

CHAPTER FOURTEEN

The Bible as We See It

*The art and orderliness of the Bible command
a respect it has not received*

The true author of the Bible was an extremely capable writer. In the preceding chapters, we have offered the merest glimpse of the depth of characterization, plot, word-play, thematic development, and literary structure found throughout the Five Books of Moses. Most of all we have shown—again, only offering a glimmer—how profoundly *unified* the text is.

A unified text implies a single author. Literary virtuosity of the kind we have shown also implies a single author, especially because the feats of authorship such as the triquad, the chiasmus, and the sevens permeate the entire text.

As to whom that author is, we are not going to jump to conclusions as the Bible critics have. We pointed out in chapter four that they do not have a scrap of physical evidence to support the idea that multiple documents were merged. Although we believe that the evidence we have presented establishes the traditional view of the Bible's unity, we do not possess any ancient copyright information in the name of Moses. All the information we possess about Moses is contained in the five books that bear his name.

The purpose of this book has been to relaunch Bible studies as a serious profession. The profession of Bible criticism as practiced at universities and divinity schools is just so nineteenth century. Clinging to a method of inquiry that is based on false, discredited, and logically incoherent premises (for example, that the different names of God imply different authors) simply does not contribute to a better understanding of the origin or meaning of the text.

Just as astrology continues to have adherents despite its demonstrated inability to explain past and present events or to predict the future, so, too, the field of Bible criticism retains a debilitating grip on Bible studies despite centuries of failure to build a useful hypothesis about the authorship of the Bible. Just as astrology is considered obsolete by modern astronomers, so, too, is Bible criticism seen as irrelevant by modern twenty-first-century Bible scholars who daily delve into the text and discover beautiful chiasmi, triquads, and Code of Seven structures and unlock coherent and compelling explanations of literary meaning.

Not only has the profession of Bible criticism been a hindrance to serious intellectual engagement with this magnificent work, it is impossible to imagine that tearing up this book has not led to lessening its authority and hence diminishing the beautiful moral lessons it offers. Apart from the problems of a secular Bible and its fragmented secular gods, of maverick ministers and renegade rabbis, the prevailing response to the Bible in modern society, particularly among the highly educated, is one of tragic indifference.

It is high time that serious people take the Bible seriously again. This is a book that speaks to the universal human condition. It is replete with moral lessons and contains a vision for how people can live spiritually elevated lives. Most of the book is focused on a journey toward a promised land, and the book's characters only arrive at its doorstep as we get to its final words. The author, through stories, themes, and literary connections, engages readers in discovering how they can get there too.

In like fashion we will trust that our readers, after weighing the evidence we present, are intelligent enough to develop their own ideas about who really wrote the Bible.

There is the antiquated and convoluted nineteenth-century view that the Bible was written by J, E, P, and D, and there is the classic alternative, both ancient and modern, that the Bible was written by a single author—let's call him M (for Mysterious or Moses, you decide).

The choice readers have is between the classic view of the Bible as a unitary text, or a vision of the Bible that rips the book into shreds. On the one hand is the traditional view that has reigned for millennia, and on the other is a notion that has come to dominate centers of professional Bible study over just a few centuries.

The Bible versus the Bible Critics

To help readers make up their minds, we will offer a final summary of the competing visions in their most condensed form. Throughout the book we have zoomed into the Bible text to show commonalities that cut across the Bible critics' alphabet of authors. Now we will look at the big picture, zooming out to see how the author took care to divide each of his five books into an introduction of some ten to twelve chapters (the first fifth of each of the five books), followed by the main story in each book.

Genesis begins with a universal history of the world, before narrowing its focus to Israelite history. Exodus starts with the history of the settlement in Egypt and the Exodus, followed by the post-Exodus desert wanderings, receiving the Torah on Mount Sinai, and building the Tabernacle. In Leviticus, we have the ground rules on the various kinds of ritual offerings and the dedication of the Tabernacle, followed by detailed instructions on how the community is to attain holiness. Numbers starts with a census and information about the arrangement of the various divisions of the Camp of Israel, with the Tabernacle now at its center; it then goes into the Israelites' journeying and the strife that prolonged their stay in the wilderness by four decades. Deuteronomy opens with a reminder of the covenant God and Israel formed at Sinai forty years earlier and lessons on trust in God; then Moses offers a detailed discussion of the laws that Israel will need to keep when they settle the Land of Israel.

STRUCTURE OF THE FIVE BOOKS OF MOSES		
BOOK	PART I	PART II
GENESIS	CHAPTERS: 1–11 Universal History: Creation, The Fall of Man, The Flood, Tower of Babel, Birth of Abraham	CHAPTERS: 12–50 Israelite History: Abraham, Isaac, Jacob, The Twelve Tribes of Israel
EXODUS	CHAPTERS: 1–12 Egyptian Exile, Moses, Ten Plagues, The Exodus	CHAPTERS: 13–40 Desert Travels, Ten Commandments, Sin of the Golden Calf, The Building of the Tabernacle
LEVITICUS	CHAPTERS: 1–10 The Operation and Dedication of the Tabernacle	CHAPTERS: 11–27 Holiness Laws Governing the Entrance to the Tabernacle; Sacrifices Outside the Tabernacle; Holiness of Man; Holiness of Time; Holiness of Space
NUMBERS	CHAPTERS: 1–10 The Census and Organization of the Israelite Camp around the Tabernacle, Travel Preparations, and Protocol	CHAPTERS: 11–36 The Desert Adventure: Sins, Complaints, Quarrels, and Disintegration of the Camp
DEUTERONOMY	CHAPTERS: 1–11 Moses' Lecture Regarding Lessons of Faith	CHAPTERS: 12–34 Moses' Lecture Regarding Practical Commandments

When we view the Bible from this global vantage point, we clearly see the internal consistency of the Bible, as well as the disciplined and detailed technique its author used. It therefore becomes undeniable that this book exhibits signs of a single, highly engaged mind.

But for sheer intensity of planning and single-minded purpose, nothing can beat the literary form of the chiasmus: it necessitates a clear vision of where something begins and where something ends; requires the author to have a clear idea of what he wants to express; and it reveals the theme through parallelisms of plot that make Shakespeare's iambic pentameter look like child's play.

Each example of this highly ordered literary form gives lie to the chaos offered by Bible criticism's source division. But seen in toto, from a big-picture perspective, not only is the Bible written in chiasmi, but the entire book is one big chiasmus:

THE PENTATEUCH CYCLE	
—1— GENESIS	—2— EXODUS
UNIVERSAL PLAN	TREK INTO THE DESERT
Creation of the World Ideal—Garden of Eden Real—Sin, Expulsion, Flood New Plan—Israel	Creation of a Nation Ideal—Covenant at Sinai Real—Rejection of the Torah New Plan—New Covenant
—3— LEVITICUS	
THE HOLINESS PLAN	
(1) Temple (2) Person (3) Time (4) Place	
—1'— DEUTERONOMY	—2'— NUMBERS
NATIONAL PLAN	TREK OUT OF THE DESERT
Formation of a Nation Ideal—Plans to Conquer Promised Land Real—Anticipation of Sin New Plan—New Commitment	Formation of a Nation Ideal—Travel Plans Real—Rejection of the Land New Plan—New Generation

The chart above shows The Pentateuch Cycle, distilling the Bible to its essence. By "cycle" we mean a sort of meta-chiasmus that shows the big picture (any of whose units may be expanded by adjusting the "lens" into more detailed chiasmi: a Genesis Cycle, an Exodus Cycle, etc.).

The book of Genesis is about God's universal plan for the world: the creation of a physical world; the spiritual possibilities of the Garden of Eden; the reality of sin, which separates earthly man from God; and God's new plan to appoint one nation to bring knowledge of God to His physical world.

The book of Exodus is parallel to the book of Genesis. Specifically, the creation of a nation is parallel to the creation of the world; the ideal of the Covenant of Sinai is parallel to the ideal of the Garden of Eden; the reality of the sin of the Golden Calf is parallel to the reality of sin and punishment (e.g., the Expulsion), both involving a rejection of God's specific instructions; each book ends with a new plan—the new covenant in Exodus, in which God agrees to stick with a sinful people by revealing his attributes of mercy, and the new nation in Genesis.

In turn, the people have to become holy, and the book of Leviticus is an instruction manual for that project. Its four elements include a place for God to dwell among the Children of Israel (the Tabernacle); the means by which they can sanctify themselves; special times (the Sabbath and holy days); and places that are outside of the Tabernacle. As with any chiasmus, its main idea is expressed in its center, and so we have in this holiness code in the book of Leviticus the unifying principle of the Bible: God created a physical arena where an earthly creature, man, can achieve spiritual heights by acting in a godly way.

The creation of a nation in Exodus is echoed in the formation of a nation in the book of Numbers; the ideal of the Torah in Exodus is echoed in the ideal of taking that holiness code to their promised land. But once again the reality of sin transforms what would have been a three-day journey into a four-decade punishment; that is because God realizes He needs a new generation to bring the Torah to the Land, just as He needed a new covenant to coexist with a sinful people in Exodus.

Finally, the book of Deuteronomy, like all the books except Leviticus, is mutually parallel within this grand chiasmus. The early development of the Children of Israel in Numbers is parallel to the advanced preparation of the Israelites who are now forty years older and ready to learn how they are to live in their new land. The ideal travel plans in Numbers have their echo in plans for conquest and settlement in Deuteronomy. The reality of sin that dominates the book of Numbers has its Deuteronomic echo in Moses' lengthy warning of what will happen if the Children of Israel fail to keep the Torah. The concluding new commitment is parallel to the new generation in Numbers: the book ends with an injunction to observe the whole Torah that Moses has taught the Children of Israel and to write it down on large stones on Mount Ebal upon crossing the Jordan into the promised land.

Much more could be said about all these mutual parallels, but we trust that the preceding graphic (or the one below) is worth at least another thousand words. The Bible distilled to its essence begins with a universal plan but ends with a national plan. In between, a group of slaves treks into the desert, receives a spiritual guidebook at Sinai, then treks out of the desert to a place it can implement the Divine revelation. The author's central purpose is quite lofty, the interlocking parallels give it strength, and the total picture is clear.

1. **Genesis**
   A failed universal plan is replaced with a national plan.
   2. **Exodus**
      God leads the nation out of the crucible of Egypt.
      ③ **LEVITICUS**
         The nation learns how to be holy.
   2.' **Numbers**
      God leads the nation to the Promised Land.
1.' **Deuteronomy**
   The nation is ready to implement its universal mission.

Now contrast our condensed vision of the Bible to that offered by the Bible critics, which in its purest distillation was handed down by the late nineteenth-century German academic Julius Wellhausen (1844–1918), the undisputed towering figure in the centuries-long history of the documentary hypothesis. Astruc may have lit the torch, and Friedman may be carrying its diminishing flame, but Wellhausen, the luminary of the field, still looms large to this day.

But what really did he say? Warning: This is not a parody!

At the core of Wellhausen's Bible was a text he called "Q" for its four (quatuor) essential covenants (Genesis 1–11). The J source was not a unity but had a complex literary history of its own, having been supplemented on two or more occasions. There was an older and a younger E, the latter of whom ran parallel to J and was particularly distinct in Genesis 20–22. The composite E was combined with a J source that had itself been interpolated several times (e.g., Genesis 12:10–20). So J was supplemented in Genesis 12–26 before being combined with E by J, a redactor distinct from the one who combined this with Q. J and E were combined so freely that R was really an author, and this *before* combining JE with Q. In fact, it was often impossible to disentangle J and E, except when the Divine name was used.

And just like J and E, Q exhibited signs of having been enlarged before being combined with both earlier and later material to form P (for example, Exodus 30–31 was added later than 25–29, but before 35–39). In fact, Wellhausen determined that Genesis 1 originally had it that the world was created in seven days, not six. (Apparently, God was working on the Sabbath in the first draft of the Torah.) What's more, the original text began with the words, "And the earth was waste and void . . ."

Wellhausen's ability to grasp the subtlest editorial changes was evidenced in his deducing that Leviticus 17–26 was older than Q but had been added to P after Q had already been incorporated in P. He even could see what was not in the text by deducing that much of Q had been excised to make room for Leviticus 17–26.

As for D, it was combined into a JE + D work prior to P since the D narrative is entirely dependent on JE and knows nothing of P (a point disputed by modern Bible critics). But Wellhausen is quick to point out that half of Numbers (N) is by someone who stood between JE and Q but was open to the outlook of JE and D.

Here's a rough graphic representation of Wellhausen's theory:[1]

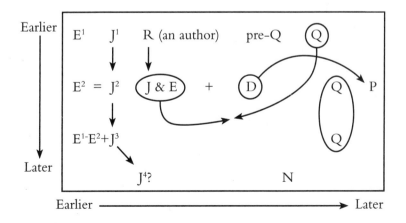

In its sheer complexity and strong elements of fantasy, Wellhausen's theory seems to share much in common with a Wagnerian opera. (The two nineteenth-century Germans also shared a penchant for anti-Semitism.)[2]

So readers have a choice: the simple elegance of the chiastic structure of the Bible, or Wellhausen's impenetrable, unverifiable self-parody. Wellhausen was a charlatan, but he must have been a powerful personality to persuade his colleagues and students to take such undisciplined speculation seriously.

One example can summarize the mess created by Wellhausen's method. First read the following verses from Exodus 14 as a straightforward description of Pharaoh's pursuit of the departing Israelites. Then marvel at what Bible critics can do with their toys:

It was told to the king of Egypt that the people had fled; and the heart of Pharaoh and his servants became transformed regarding the people, and they said, "What is this that we have done that we have sent away Israel from serving us?" He harnessed his chariot and attracted his people with him. He took six hundred elite chariots and all the chariots of Egypt, with officers on them all. Hashem strengthened the heart of Pharaoh, king of Egypt, and he pursued the Children of Israel—and the Children of Israel were going out with an upraised arm. Egypt pursued them and overtook them, encamped by the sea—all the horses and chariots of Pharaoh, and his horsemen and army—by Pi-hahiroth before Baal-zephon. Pharaoh approached; the Children of Israel raised their eyes and behold!—Egypt was journeying after them, and they were very frightened; the Children of Israel cried out to Hashem. (Exodus 14)

Key: J-*E*-P

It was told to the king of Egypt that the people had fled; *and the heart of Pharaoh and his servants became transformed regarding the people, and they said, "What is this that we have done that we have sent away Israel from serving us?"* **He harnessed his chariot and attracted his people with him. He took six hundred elite chariots and all the chariots of Egypt, with officers on them all.** Hashem strengthened the heart of Pharaoh, king of Egypt, and he pursued the Children of Israel—and the Children of Israel were going out with an upraised arm. **Egypt pursued them** and overtook them, encamped by the sea—all the horses and chariots of Pharaoh, and his horsemen and army—by Pi-Hahiroth before Baal-Zephon. Pharaoh approached; **the Children of Israel raised their eyes and behold!—Egypt was journeying after them, and they were very frightened;** the Children of Israel cried out to Hashem.

We believe the time has come to stop ripping up the Bible and start trying to understand it. The principle of Occam's razor suggests that between two approaches the best explanation is the one that says the most with the least, not the one that yields a twisted flowchart driven by an arbitrary and constantly changing complex set of rules.

Passing Fads

The truth is that biblical criticism is nothing more than a passing fad. It was fashionable in the eighteenth century to question whether *The Iliad* and *The Odyssey* were really written by one man named Homer and propose instead that they derived from earlier sources that underwent a process of canonization at a later date.[3]

Sound familiar? It was in this intellectual climate that Astruc developed his ideas on multiple authorship of the Bible.

It was not only literary fads that influenced the original Bible critics. Another fad which Bible critics from Wellhausen to Friedman unconsciously echo is the Marxist notion of a ruling class that—through its control of the means of production—conditions social, political, and economic life.

So it is little surprise that Wellhausen's theory focuses on the triumph of P, which represented an aristocratic priestly class that lived parasitically off the religion-based (read: "opiate of the masses") sacrifices (read: royal banquets) of the Israelites. To gain legitimacy, P back-projected the ruling class's system of privileges to Mosaic times, using Chronicles and his re-written Bible to support this. Not even Karl Marx took more seriously the idea that history is literally written by the victors. According to Wellhausen, the supposed history of the Israelites was a myth used to justify fifth-century BCE power politics.

Modern Bible critics like Friedman do the same thing. While he states in his book that Jewish life in Temple times was above all else influenced by religion, he is constantly citing crass political motivations for P rewriting an earlier Bible to support the political interests of the "Aaronid" ruling class against its pro-Moses rivals. (Remember, this notion of a Shilo priesthood devoted to their ancestor Moses is pure fiction).

Homeric criticism and Marxist theory have fallen by the wayside, but the fad of Bible criticism remains long overdue for the dustbin of history. As we stated earlier, we cannot say much about who M was. But if you accept that he was one author who published his work at an early stage of Israelite history—the traditional view, which centuries of Bible criticism have not succeeded in supplanting as our book has shown—then his history had to be right, or his book would have been dismissed. Why else would the nation of Israel (no slouches in the intellectual history of the world) have bought into M's book and launched its appearance on international bestseller lists from that early time until now?

We have detailed the circuitous routes of illogic pursued by the Bible critics; we have exposed Bible criticism's utter vacuity and uselessness as a theory. At the same time, we have presented a picture of the Bible's pristine coherence, a matchless unity of structure and content. If you accept our view, which really just spells out the traditional view, then the implications are clear. It is time to start taking the Bible seriously.

More on the Names of God

In chapter five, we explained how a great many sophisticated people with advanced degrees somehow permit themselves to misconstrue something as basic as the difference between a name (Hashem) and a title (Elokim).

In order to avoid getting sidetracked, we limited our analysis to what was necessary to undermine the central pillar of the Bible critics' hypothesis, but much more should be said to expose their mistakes with respect to the names of God.

Specifically, in a case of scholarly malpractice, the Bible critics misunderstand three significant Bible texts pertaining to the use of the names of God. First, a little review of their argument:

In the beginning, J refers to God as Hashem, and P and E use Elokim. (The age order of J, E, P, and D does not correspond to the narrative chronology of the Bible, for which R is given credit). Therefore, whenever Hashem appears in the book of Genesis—J is the author; if Elokim is used, the author must either be E or P. (And scholars using advanced critical methods determine if the biblical author is E or P.)

This pattern goes on until the book of Exodus, where the rules change as follows: From Exodus 3, E begins using Hashem as well as Elokim, and from Exodus 6, P begins doing the same. From then on, E and P can use either name, but J still uses only Hashem.

But what prompted this major change? The Bible critics contend that there were three differing and contradictory traditions regarding the name of God. For J, Hashem was always the name of God. This is why J authored the following verse:

"And as for Seth, to him also a son was born, and he named him Enosh. Then men began to call upon the name Hashem." (Genesis 4:26)

J, therefore, not only refers to God as Hashem in his narrative, he even puts the name Hashem into the mouths of biblical characters such as Abraham. J simply assumed that this name was always known.

In contrast, E and P believed that the name Hashem was totally unknown before the Exodus, and therefore refused to use the name Hashem until that point, even in their narration. So when do they actually begin using the name Hashem? Here is where they differ. E took it from the well-known story of the burning bush, when Moses first meets God and is charged with taking the Israelites out of Egypt (a passage that, of course, E himself authored):

Moses said to God: "Behold, when I come to the Children of Israel and say to them:

'The God of your forefathers has sent me to you,' and they say to me: 'What is His Name?'—what shall I say to them?"

Hashem answered Moses: "I Shall Be As I Shall Be."

And He said: "So shall you say to the Children of Israel: 'I Shall Be has sent me to you.'"

God said further to Moses: "So shall you say to the Children of Israel: '**Hashem** the God of your forefathers, the God of Abraham, the God of Isaac, and the God of

Jacob has dispatched me to you. This is My Name forever, and this is My remembrance from generation to generation.' Go and gather the elders of Israel and say to them: '**Hashem**, the God of your forefathers, has appeared to me, the God of Abraham, Isaac, and Jacob,' saying: 'I have surely remembered you and what is done to you in Egypt.'" (Exodus 3:13–16)

Three chapters later, P follows E in using the name Hashem. First, a little background: After the burning bush episode, Moses indeed heads down to Egypt, and while successful at convincing the Israelites that God sent him to save them, his mission to Pharaoh is a debacle. Pharaoh punishes the freedom-seeking Israelites with an increased workload. Moses protests to God, Who answers as follows in this classic P text:

God spoke to Moses and said to him: "I am Hashem. **I appeared to Abraham, to Isaac and to Jacob as E-L Sha-dai, but with My Name Hashem I did not make Myself known to them**. Moreover, I established My covenant with them to give them the land of Canaan, the land of their sojourning, in which they sojourned. Moreover, I have heard the groan of the Children of Israel whom Egypt enslaves and I have remembered My covenant. Therefore, say to the Children of Israel—'I am Hashem, and I shall take you out from under the burdens of Egypt; I shall rescue you from their service; I shall redeem you with an outstretched arm and with great judgments. I shall take you to Me for a people and I shall be a God to you; and you shall know that I am Hashem your God, Who takes you out from under the burdens of Egypt. I shall bring you to the land about which I raised My hand to give it to Abraham, Isaac, and Jacob; and I shall give it to you as a heritage—I am Hashem.'" (Exodus 6:2–8)

In the Bible critics' understanding, Hashem was not known to the forefathers in P. Hence, J must have written all the passages in Genesis that mention Hashem.

But this theory raises many more troubling questions than it answers:

1. When, according to P, did Moses get assigned the role of savior? Did P not know of the famous burning bush episode?
2. How did three different and even contradictory notions regarding the history of the name of God develop in ancient Israelite society?
3. How could the editor R not have realized this terrible contradiction regarding which name of God was known at what time?
4. If R did realize it, why did he or she or they not eliminate this contradiction from the final version of the Bible?
5. Bible critics say that Hashem's name was introduced in J's Genesis 4:26, after the birth of Enosh ("Then men began to call upon the name Hashem"). Yet Eve, generations earlier, says the following: "Now the man had known his wife Eve, and she conceived and bore Cain, saying: 'I have acquired a man with Hashem.'" (Genesis 4:1) The story of Adam and Eve is classic J; shouldn't documentary hypothesists know their own major documents?
6. Even if E and P assumed that the forefathers had not known about the name Hashem, what would stop them from using this name? At the very least, why could they not use this name as part of the narration of the stories of Genesis?
7. This notion that E will never use Hashem before Exodus 3 is

simply not true. Take a look at the following E passage:

Then Jacob took a vow, saying: "If God will be with me, will guard me on this way that I am going; will give me bread to eat and clothes to wear, and I return in peace to my father's house, and **Hashem** will be a God to me, then this stone which I have set up as a pillar shall become a house of God, and whatever You will give me, I shall surely tithe to You."(Genesis 28:20–22)

To which Richard E. Friedman unapologetically notes:

"This is one of only three occurrences in the Torah in which the name of God appears in a source other than J prior to the revelation of the name to Moses in Exodus." [1]

Another is the following P source:

"And Hashem did for Sarah as He had spoken."(Genesis 21:1) The Bible critics have a high tolerance for exceptions to their own rules.

USE OF THE DIVINE NAMES IN THE BOOK OF GENESIS		
J USES "HASHEM"	*E* USES "ELOKIM"	P USES "ELOKIM"
"And as for Seth, to him also a son was born, and he named him Enosh. Then men began to call upon the name 'Hashem.'" (Genesis 4:26)	Mainly Elokim	Mainly Elokim

J USES HASHEM	E BEGINS USING HASHEM	P BEGINS USING "HASHEM"
As above	*"Moses said to God: 'Behold, when I come to the Children of Israel and say to them: The God of your forefathers has sent me to you, and they say to me: What is His Name?—what shall I say to them?'* "**HASHEM** *answered Moses: 'I Shall Be As I Shall Be . . .'"* (Exodus 3:13–16)	"God spoke to Moses and said to him: 'I am Hashem. I appeared to Abraham, to Isaac and to Jacob as E-L Sha-dai, but with My Name **HASHEM** I did not make Myself known to them. . . .'" (Exodus 6:2–8)

THE USE OF THE DIVINE NAMES IN THE BOOK OF EXODUS

We posit that the Bible critics did not understand the meaning of these three passages, which they offer as crucial proof of multiple authorship of the Bible (because they believe "Hashem" is being introduced as a new name in Exodus, though it is used repeatedly in Genesis).

Let us review each of these three passages in turn:

". . . Then men began to call upon the name Hashem." (Genesis 4:26)

The Bible critics see this statement as a first historical turning point in the knowledge of God's name. Their point is to draw attention to the fact that, according to J's understanding, it was the third generation of humanity that began to acknowledge Hashem; this is supposed to be at odds with E's and P's understanding. In fact, however, they mistranslate the text, which should be understood as follows:

". . . Then the calling in the name of Hashem began to be profaned."

The Hebrew word for "began" in this instance is *huchal*, an idiom that in the Bible always means the beginning of something negative. Here are five illustrations:

"And it came to pass when Man began (*hechel*) to increase upon the ground and daughters were born to them. . . ." [Then powerful rulers just took the women they desired as wives.] (Genesis 6:1)

"Noah, the man of the earth, debased (*vayachel*) himself and planted a vineyard." (Genesis 9:20)

"And Cush begot Nimrod. He was the first (*hachel*) to be a mighty man on earth." (Genesis 10:8)

"And Hashem said: 'Behold, they are one people with one language for all, and this they begin (*hachilam*) to do! And now, should it not be withheld from them all they propose to do?'" (Genesis 11:6)

"Israel settled in the Shittim and the people began (*vayachel*) to commit harlotry with the daughters of Moab." (Numbers 25:1)

In each of the above verses, the root h-ch-l (in Hebrew, most words are constructed from a three-letter root) signifies the beginning of something bad.

So for the Bible critics who translate the verse as ". . . Then men began to call upon the name Hashem," the question is: why would the Bible use a term that implies that this was a negative development in human history?[2]

Elsewhere in the Bible, Ezekiel uses h-ch-l in a prophecy of the end of days, directly quoting God:

I will make known my holy Name among My people Israel, and I will nevermore desecrate (*achel*) My holy Name, and the nations shall know that I am Hashem, the holy One in Israel. (Ezekiel: 39:7)

From the context it is clear that the only acceptable definition for h–ch–l is to profane or to desecrate. Jewish tradition has always understood Genesis 4:26 as a reference to the generation that initiated idol worship. It is from the generation of Enosh that man profaned God's Name by ascribing to other entities in the world the qualities and powers that are God's alone. And Ezekiel provides the bookend, prophesying that the world will be filled with knowledge of Hashem, Who himself will no longer allow His Name to be profaned.

Now let's take a look at Exodus 3, from which the Bible critics derive the notion that the forefathers had not known Hashem's personal name. The meaning of the passage should rather be understood as follows:

"Moses said to God: 'Behold, when I come to the Children of Israel and say to them: The God of your forefathers has sent me to you,' and they say to me: 'What is his Name?'—what shall I say to them?'"

Explanation: Because the Children of Israel have been living in Egypt for generations, surrounded by idolaters and arguably the most densely populated pantheon of gods of all ancient peoples and civilizations—each god possessing specific qualities and natures—they will ask me to explain this God's nature. So what shall I tell them?

Hashem answered Moses: "I shall be as I shall be (*eheyeh asher eheyeh*)."

God answers: I have no definable character as I transcend nature. I am what I am, eternal and incorporeal.

And He said: "So shall you say to the Children of Israel: 'I Shall Be (*eheyeh*) has sent me to you.'"

God goes on: Tell the children of Israel that this God has no definite nature—but even so, He has interest in human affairs, especially theirs.

God said further to Moses: "So shall you say to the Children of Israel: 'Hashem the God of your forefathers, the God of Abraham, the God of Isaac, and the God of Jacob has dispatched me to you. This is My Name forever, and this is My remembrance from generation to generation.'"

After God explains His undefinable nature and deflects any pagan notion of Himself, He retreats back to the original question and offers an actual name. And the name is Hashem—the God of Israel's ancestors.

> Go and gather the elders of Israel and say to them: "Hashem, the God of your forefathers, has appeared to me, the God of Abraham, Isaac, and Jacob," saying: "I have surely remembered you and what is done to you in Egypt." (Exodus 3:13–16)

From this last statement it is self-evident that the elders of Israel were familiar with the name Hashem and that this was the God of their forefathers—for otherwise they would have no idea what and about whom Moses was talking, dismissing him as an old and blubbering fool.

So we are left with Exodus 6, which seems to imply that Hashem was not known to the forefathers. But that is only what it seems to those who split up the Bible into various sources and assign them to different authors. Those who read the stories of Genesis as a coherent whole would have no problem at all. Let us take a closer look at this verse:

> God spoke to Moses and said to him: "I am Hashem. I appeared to Abraham, to Isaac, and to Jacob as E-L Shadai, but with My Name Hashem I did not make Myself known to them." (Exodus 6:2–3)

Notice the shift from "appeared" to "known." For the sake of consistency, the verse should have read as follows:

". . . I *appeared* to Abraham, to Isaac, and to Jacob as E-L Sha-dai, but with My Name Hashem I did not make Myself *appear* to them."

Or, the other way around:

". . . I was *known* to Abraham, to Isaac, and to Jacob as E-L Sha-dai, but with My Name Hashem I did not make Myself *known* to them."

Because the Bible uses language so precisely, the use of two different verbs where one would normally suffice is meant to tell us something. And, indeed, in the context of a Bible that is read as a complete story, we know that the name Hashem appeared to the forefathers. But the verse is pointedly clarifying only that the name was not known to them.

This begs the question—what is the difference between the two? And the answer is fairly straightforward: An appearance is purely superficial, whereas to be known—in the biblical sense—implies either an intimate bonding, or a realization of some sort (just as in English the word "realize" implies both cognition as well as the attainment of a final product or goal).

In other words: The name E-L Sha-dai not only appeared to the forefathers but was actually realized, whereas the name Hashem, although it appeared, was not realized. To what does this refer? What was not realized? It is here that a little knowledge of Genesis comes in handy. It is well known that God promised the forefathers two things: a great nation, and a land (Canaan).

There are two specific times that God makes the promise of land: in chapter 15 of Genesis to Abraham and in chapter 28 to Jacob. In both of these instances, God appears to the forefathers in a vision or a dream as Hashem; hence the Bible critics assume J to be the author of these passages. And twice God makes promises regarding nationhood or seed:[3] in chapter 17 to Abraham and in chapter 35 to Jacob. In both of these instances, God appears as E-L Sha-dai; hence the Bible critics assume P to be the author of these passages. The table sums it up:

DIVINE PROMISES TO THE FOREFATHERS			
E-L Sha-dai			
CHAPTER	PERSON	PROMISE	SOURCE
Genesis 17	Abraham	Seed	P
Genesis 35	Jacob	Seed	P
Hashem			
CHAPTER	PERSON	PROMISE	SOURCE
Genesis 15	Abraham	Land	J
Genesis 28	Jacob	Land	J

Based on this background information, we can now understand our verse in Exodus 6. Remember that Moses complained to God that his first meeting with Pharaoh was a failure: the burdens only increased and freedom seemed more distant than ever. To which God responded (and we paraphrase): "Moses, I have made two promises to your forefathers, one regarding their seed becoming a great nation, and the other regarding their own territory and country. Note that I have come through with the nation part, and, admittedly, not with the land. But now I come to fulfill that part of My promise." In other words, what God has promised through the name E-L Sha-dai, namely nationhood, was realized (made known), but what was promised in the name Hashem, the land, has not yet been realized (made known). Hence our verse reads as follows:

> God spoke to Moses and said to him: "I am Hashem. I appeared to Abraham, to Isaac, and to Jacob as E-L Sha-dai (and I fulfilled that promise), but with My Name Hashem I did not make Myself known to them (for I did not fulfill that promise yet)."

But God continues:

> "I established My covenant with them to give them the land of Canaan, the land of their sojourning, in which they sojourned."

It is now time to come through with the promise of the land, and hence the Exodus is near (and not ever more distant as feared because of Pharaoh's punitive reaction to Moses' demand).

The emptiness and confusion of the multiple authorship theory is all the more apparent because the above explanation has been known for about seven hundred years. It was first pointed out by a medieval Bible commentator named Rabbi Yaakov ben Asher (1269–1343), known as the Baal HaTurim, and further popularized by Umberto Cassuto in his commentary on Exodus.

Maybe it is the Baal HaTurim's lack of literary and historical skills or Cassuto's absence from the preferred scholarly journals and conferences that could account for Bible critic Richard Elliott Friedman opening one of his books with this statement:[4]

> [No one] has ever responded to the classic and current arguments that made the documentary hypothesis the central model. . . .

The great scientist Sir Isaac Newton famously remarked: "If I have seen further [than other men] it is by standing upon the shoulders of giants." Newton understood that his great achievements in physics depended on the work of Galileo and Kepler before him. The Bible critics in contrast have shown themselves prone to many avoidable errors because they routinely sidestep sages who have achieved monumental levels of scholarship before them.

More on the Code

As we learned in chapter 13, the Code of Seven is woven throughout the text of the Torah. The list below includes a sample of seven codes appearing in just the books of Genesis and Exodus. A comprehensive list for the whole Torah would be too long to include, but this list illustrates just how pervasive the seven codes are.

GENESIS

CHAPTER 1: Creation (P)

35—אלקים—God

21—ארץ—Earth

14—מים—Water

7—ויהי כן—And It Was So

7—טוב—Good

2–3: Garden of Eden (J)

21—איש-אשה—Man, Woman

14—עץ—Tree

7—טוב—Good

7—אדמה—Soil

7—שדה—Field

4: Cain and Abel (J)

7—אח—Brother

**5–6: "Begats" or
"This is the history of . . ."
(R or P & J)**

7—אלקים—God

6–7–8: Flood (J-P)

35—נח—Noah

9: Rainbow covenant (P)

7—ברית—Covenant

12: Introduction to Abram (J)

7—אברם—Abram

12–13: Abram and Sarai in Egypt (J)

14—אברם—Abram

7—מצרים—Egypt

7—י-ה-ו-ה—Hashem

7—אשת—Wife

15: Covenant of eternal protection (J)

7—י-ה-ו-ה—Hashem

16: Story of Hagar (J-P)

7—הגר—Hagar

17: Covenant of circumcision (P)

7—זרע—Seed

18–19: Sodom and Gomorrah (J)

7—סדם—Sodom

7—צדיק—Righteous

7—מצא—Find

21: Birth of Isaac (E-P)

7—יצחק—Isaac

21: Alliance of Abraham and Abimelech (E)

7—אברהם—Abraham

7—אבימלך—Abimelech

22: Binding of Isaac (E-R)

7—ירא—Fear, Seeing

24: Abraham acquires a wife for Isaac (J)

14—אברהם—Abraham

14—קח—Acquire

26: Confrontation of Isaac and Abimelech (J)

7—אבימלך—Abimelech

7—חפר—Dig

25–27: Double struggle over the birthright (J-P)

7—בכר—Firstborn

27–28: Stealing of the birthright (J-P)

28—ברך—Bless

21—יעקב—Jacob

7—רבקה—Rebecca

29: Jacob meets Rachel at the well (J)

7—באר—Well

29: Jacob at the well (J)

7—אח—Brother

29: Jacob becomes a servant of Laban (J)

7—עבד—Servant

29–30: Leah the matriarch (J-E)

14—לאה—Leah

30: Jacob amasses wealth (J)

14—צאן—Flock

31: Jacob's real brothers (J-E-P)

7—אח—Brother

32–33: Jacob and Esau reconcile (J-E)

14—עשו—Esau

7—אדני—My Master

7—אח—Brother

7—ישתחו—Bow

34: Jacob's daughter and the city of Shechem (J)

7—בת—Daughter

7—עיר—City

35: Journey to Beth El (E-P)

7—בית א-ל—Beth El

36: Descendants and chiefs of Esau (P-J)

42—אלוף—Chief

37: Confrontation of Joseph and his brothers (J-E)

21—אח—Brother

14—יוסף—Joseph

38: Judah repents, the twins' hand (J)

7—אח—Brother

7—יד—Hand

39: The slander of Joseph (J)

7—דבר—Speech

40: Joseph solves dreams, lifting of the head (E)

7—פטר—Solve

7—ראש—Head

41: Joseph predicts the famine in Egypt (E)

14—מצרים—Egypt

7—רעב—Famine

7—פטר—Solve

7—חלום—Dream

41–42: Providing provisions during the famine (E-J)

7—רעב—Famine

7—שבר—Provision

42: Joseph accuses his brothers (E-J)

7—מרגלים—Spies

7—אחיכם—Your Brother

7—אב—Father

43: The brothers struggle with Jacob (J-E)

14—אב—Father

44: Jacob tricks his brothers (J)

7—אמתחת—Sacks

7—עבד—Slave

44: Judah pleads on behalf of Benjamin (J)

7—אדני—My Master

7—נער—Lad

14—אב—Father

21—עבד—Servant

45: Joseph reunites with his 12 brothers (J-E)

14—יוסף—Joseph

21—אח—Brother

46: Census of the children of Israel (P)
7—אלה—These are
21—בני—Sons of

46–47: The land of Goshen (J)
7—גשן—Goshen

47: Acquiring land for their cattle (J)
7—מקנה—Cattle
7—אדמה—Land

48: Final blessings (P-E)
7—ברך—Bless

49–50: Burial of Jacob (P-J)
14—קבר—Bury
21—אביו—His Father

50: Death of Joseph (J-E)
7—יוסף—Joseph

EXODUS

Chapter 1: Introduction (R-J-P)
70 People
Seven Expressions of Israel's Population Growth

1: Israelites multiply and the midwives are hired (E)
7—Occurrences of "Multiply"
7—מילדת—Midwives

2: Moses is born (J)
7—הילד—The Lad

1–2: Israel is enslaved (P)
7—עבד—Slave

2: Moses matures (J)
7—משה—Moses
7—איש—Man

3–4: Moses at the burning bush (J-E)
14—משה—Moses
14—ראה—Revelation, See, Fear

4–5–6: Aaron (E-J)
7—אהרן—Aaron

7: Nile turns to blood (E-P)
14—יאור—Nile
7—מצרים—Egypt
Seven Days Before Next Plague

7–8: Frogs (E-P)
7—משה—Moses
Seven Locations of the Plague

8: Wild beasts (E)
7—ערב—Swarm of Wild Beasts

9: Hashem destroys the fields with hail (E)
14—י-ה-ו-ה—Hashem
14—ברד—Hail
7—שדה—Field
7—משה—Moses (E-R—last sentence)

10: Locusts (E)
7—ארבה—Locust
7—משה—Moses

11: Pharaoh's final warning (E-R)
7—פרעה—Pharaoh

12: The new moon & paschal lamb (P-J-E)
7—חדש—Month, New
7—ראש—First, Head
7—ישראל—Israel
14—אכל—Eat
7—דם—Blood

14: Pharaoh chases after Israel (J-P)
7—ישראל—Israel
7—פרעה—Pharaoh

14: Egypt is drowned (J-P)
7—ים—Sea
14—מצרים—Egypt

15–16: Stories regarding water (J-E-R)
7—מים—Water

17: Complaints of the nation (R-E)
7—העם—The Nation

17: Hands of Moses defeat Amalek (E)

7—עמלק—Amalek

7—יד—Hand

7—משה—Moses

18: Moses' father-in-law (E)

7—יתרו—Yitro

7—חתן משה—Father-in-Law of Moses

19: Preparation for the revelation at Sinai (J-E)

14—משה—Moses

7—עלה—Ascend

7—ירד—Descend

19–20: Revelation of Sinai (J-E-P)

7—קל—Voice

7—ירא—Fear, Seeing

21: Release of a slave (E)

7—יצא—Go Free

21: Laws between people (E)

14—איש-אשה-אנשים—Man, Woman, Men

21: Laws between people (E)

14—מת—Kill

21: Laws between people (E)

7—שור—Ox

21–22: Obligations to your fellow (E)

7—רעהו—His Fellow

21–22: Restitution (E)

7—שלם—Pay

24: Moses ascends the mountain (E-P)
14—משה—Moses
7—ישראל—Israel
7—עלה—Ascend

25: Covering of the Ark (P)
7—כפרת—Cover

27–28: Aaron's special garments (P)
7—אהרן—Aaron

34: Tablets (J-R-P)
7—לחת—Tablets

35: The contributions of the heart (P)
7—לב—Heart
7—תרומה—Contribution
14—בוא—Come Forth, Bring Forth

35–36: The wise builders of the Tabernacle (P)
7—חכם—Wise

25–40: Contributions to the Tabernacle (P)
7—נדב—Generous (25:2)
21—לב—Heart

ENDNOTES

PART I

CHAPTER ONE

1. Dennis Prager, "Faith in Exodus," *The Jewish Journal* (April 19, 2001), www.jewishjournal.com/religion/article/faith_in_exodus_20010420/.
2. For a comprehensive and clear explanation of the laws commanding capital punishment, see Rabbi Joseph Telushkin, *Biblical Literacy* (New York: William Morrow, 1997), 405-408. Telushkin cites and provides context for Genesis 9:6; Exodus 21:12, 21:14, and 21:20; Leviticus 24:17; Numbers 35:16, 35:31, and 35:33; Deuteronomy 19:11-13, 19:19-20, and 24:7.

CHAPTER TWO

1. Thomas Hobbes (1588–1679) is best known for his belief in the need for authoritarian government to prevent perpetual conflict among people left in a state of nature. Benedict Spinoza (1632–1677), born into the Judeo–Portuguese community of Amsterdam (his Hebrew name was Baruch), was regarded as a heretic and excommunicated.
2. Spinoza was not the first Bible critic to suggest Ezra, the post-exilic leader who lived in the fourth century BCE. In 1574, Andreas Masius suggested Ezra in his commentary on the book of Joshua.
3. *Stanford Encyclopedia of Philosophy*, http://plato.stanford.edu/entries/spinoza/#2.
4. Two others besides Jean Astruc were given credit for independently

coming up with this theory: H. B. Witter and J. G. Eichhorn. All three lived in the eighteenth century. Although Witter was the first to suggest it, his book was not noticed, so Astruc is generally credited with father-ing the idea and Eichhorn with heightening its respectability (since he was a professional Bible scholar).

5. The Tetragrammaton, God's holiest name, was not to be used profanely. Indeed, so strict have Jews been in respectfully refraining from its non-sacral use that even today no one knows for sure how to pronounce this name. Religious Jews say *Ado-nai,* meaning "the Lord," in prayer, and "Hashem" in ordinary speech.

6. Jews traditionally render God's names as we do here when not using them for sacral purposes, as in prayer. *Elokim* in Hebrew would actually be transliterated as *Elo-him.*

7. It was Eichhorn who first named the sources by the first German initial of the Divine name used in the biblical text.

8. Richard Elliott Friedman, *Who Wrote the Bible?* (New York: Harper and Row, 1997), 50–51.

9. References throughout this book to "Bible critics," "historical criti-cism," etc., are in no way meant as terms of disparagement. The field of biblical criticism is the academic treatment of the Bible as a historical document and "Bible critics" is the accepted term for scholars engaged in this field.

10. Ibid., 52–53.

11. John Rogerson, *Old Testament Criticism in the Nineteenth Century: Eng-land and Germany* (London: SPCK/Fortress, 1985), 42–43.

12. The chapter numbers were assigned many years after the actual canon-ization of the Bible.

CHAPTER THREE

1. Rowan Williams, *Writing in the Dust, After September 11* (Grand Rapids, MI: Eerdmans Publishing Company, 2002).

2. Brian Ross and Rehab El-Buri, "Obama's Pastor: God Damn America, U.S. to Blame for 9/11," ABC News, http://abcnews.go.com/Blotter/DemocraticDebate/story?id=4443788&page=1, (March 13, 2008).

3. Throughout this book, we use ArtScroll's translation of the Torah text because it is accessible and clear. In many instances, though, we have freely translated the Torah text ourselves or chosen alternative transla-tions where we felt that would lead to greater clarity. We gratefully

acknowledge ArtScroll's permission and recommend *The Chumash: The Stone Edition*, ArtScroll series, (Brooklyn: Mesorah Publications, 1998).

CHAPTER FOUR

1. Richard Elliott Friedman, *Who Wrote the Bible?* (New York: Harper and Row, 1997), 28.
2. Ibid., 261.
3. To the contrary, after the monarchy splits, the northern kingdom's spiritual (i.e., idolatrous) centers resided in Beit El and Dan, and the Bible specifically records that the new northern king, Jeroboam, "cast out" the Levites and replaced them with priests "who were not of the sons of Levi" (1 Kings 12:31). The second book of Chronicles, 11:5–17, specifically states:

   > Rehoboam lived in Jerusalem and built up towns for defense in Judah . . .The priests and Levites from all their districts throughout Israel sided with him. The Levites even abandoned their pasture lands and property, and came to Judah and Jerusalem because Jeroboam and his sons had rejected them as priests of Hashem. And he appointed his own priests for the high places and for the goat and calf idols he had made. Those from every tribe of Israel who set their hearts on seeking Hashem, the God of Israel, followed the Levites to Jerusalem to offer sacrifices to Hashem, the God of their fathers. They strengthened the kingdom of Judah and supported Rehoboam, son of Solomon for three years, walking in the ways of David and Solomon for three years.

   See also: 2 Chronicles 13:9–10. Nowhere do we find a group of descendants of Moses in the north or south of the ancient Jewish kingdom.
4. Although we could go through all five books of the Torah and point out the narrative gaps in the various "sources," we have limited ourselves in this discussion to the book of Genesis and the beginning of Exodus because the documentary hypothesis is rooted in these sections.
5. Richard Elliott Friedman, *The Bible with Sources Revealed* (San Francisco: HarperOne, 2003), 126.

CHAPTER FIVE

1. Numbers 22:2–24:25.
2. Only once in the Five Books of Moses, in the plague of hail (Exodus 9:30), does the compound name Hashem-Elokim appear.
3. Richard Elliott Friedman, *Who Wrote the Bible?* (New York: Harper and Row, 1997), 44, 80, 122.
4. We limit this discussion to Genesis because the entire documentary hypothesis is founded on the book of Genesis.
5. Umberto Cassuto, *The Documentary Hypothesis* (Jerusalem: Shalem Press, 2006).

PART II

CHAPTER SIX

1. Richard Elliott Friedman, *The Bible with Sources Revealed* (San Francisco: HarperOne, 2003), 11.
2. Ibid., 12.
3. The necromancers (and Aaron) do make an appearance again in the plague of boils (Exodus 9:8:12). The text there mentions that the plague afflicted every Egyptian, including the necromancers who "could not stand before Moses because of the boils." They were in the story but could not even attempt their magic, so Aaron was once again in the story to preserve symmetry.
4. Ironically, for all their love of Aaron's staff and magic, it is Moses who with his own staff performs the greatest miracle of all, the parting of the Sea of Reeds, and that is a P story. This is a major contradiction of the Bible critics' hypothesis. If Moses is the hero, it should then be an E story. Though the critics could not avoid giving that story to P for other reasons, they do give two other stories involving Aaron's staff to P as well. But both those stories, Korach's rebellion (Numbers 16–17) and the rebellious generation (Numbers 20), involved challenges to authority. In Numbers 17:25, God specifically ordered that Aaron's staff be used as a sign against would-be rebels. So the two stories in no way provide evidence of P, since even if there were a hundred stories involving a challenge to authority, one would expect the use of Aaron's staff every time, no matter who wrote it.

CHAPTER SEVEN

1. See: Richard Elliott Friedman, *The Bible with Sources Revealed* (San Francisco: HarperOne, 2003), for a coded division of the entire Torah according to a consensus view of Bible critics.
2. This verse is slightly different in its wording than the others. It says "book of the history of man" rather than just "history of man." The meaning is the same.
3. We use Umberto Cassuto's brilliant translation for this excerpt. See: Umberto Cassuto, *The Documentary Hypothesis* (Jerusalem/New York: Shalem Press, 2006).
4. *Etz Hayim*, the authoritative Torah and commentary of Judaism's Conservative movement, and the contemporary Bible critics Nahum Sarna, Robert Alter, and Richard Elliott Friedman all divide Genesis 2:4 in half. Friedman says that R rather than P wrote 2:4a and that J wrote 2:4b; either way, the verse is torn asunder.
5. A final and fourth problem with the splitting of Genesis 2:4 is of a mechanical nature. Look at any Torah scroll in the world and you will see consistency in its layout. Getting even one letter wrong, or breaking up paragraphs improperly, would invalidate a Torah scroll. Yet according to Bible critics, 2:4a was somehow detached from a preceding paragraph and attached to the following paragraph, which had inexplicably begun with a sentence fragment.
6. See the final footnote in Richard Elliott Friedman, *The Bible with Sources Revealed* (San Francisco: HarperOne, 2003), beginning on page 130.
7. Friedman, *Who Wrote the Bible?* (New York: Harper and Row, 1997), 219, 230.

CHAPTER EIGHT

1. A straightforward reading of the text makes clear that the "first account" presents the big picture of God's creation of the world and the "second account" zooms in on the story of man; it's only one story, not two competing accounts.
2. Richard Elliott Friedman, *The Bible with Sources Revealed* (San Francisco: HarperOne, 2003), 2.
3. In general, punning involves words that have the same root, but vocalization and tense changes may make this less than obvious in English

transliteration. For example, *eid* may not sound like *adamah* or *adam* to an English speaker, but these words are obviously connected to a Hebrew speaker. The first word is spelled "aleph-daled," the second word is spelled "aleph-daled-mem-hay," and the third word is spelled "aleph-daled-mem." If these were English words, they would look like: A-D, A-D-M-A, and A-D-M. The relationship among these is clear, especially as the meanings are related: "from deep" [below], "ground," and "man" [who was formed from the earth].

4. See: Exodus 19:10–11 for another J example.
5. See: Genesis 35:1 for another E example.
6. See: Genesis 9:1–6, 15–16 for other P examples.
7. See: Deuteronomy 5:6–11 for another D example.
8. There are numerous translations of the Hebrew *lech lecha*, such as "go for your own self." We follow Cassuto's translation, which seems to avoid awkwardness in English while correctly implying a sense of personal mission. See: Umberto Cassuto, *From Noah to Abraham* (Jerusalem: The Hebrew University Magnes Press, 1964), 309.
9. The settlement of Shechem can be found in Genesis 33:18–20.
10. Robert Alter, *Genesis: Translation and Commentary* (New York: W. W. Norton & Co., 1997), xli.
11. Richard Elliott Friedman, *The Bible with Sources Revealed* (San Francisco: HarperOne, 2003), 83–84.
12. Ibid.
13. Ibid.

CHAPTER NINE

1. In Hebrew, as in English, one would normally say, "accept my gift" (*ve'lakachta minchati*). In fact, Jacob says exactly that just one verse earlier (33:10) as he builds up to his real point, making good on his illicit taking of the blessing a generation earlier.
2. This is how Richard Elliott Friedman divides the sources in *Who Wrote the Bible?*, 250. It should be noted, however, that in his later book, *The Bible with Sources Revealed*, 139, he changes his mind, giving Exodus 12:22–23 to E. Apparently, the verdict is still out on the source of this passage.
3. Rabbi Menachem Leibtag of the Tanach Study Center astutely notes these parallels: See: http://www.tanach.org/shmot/kitisa/kitisas1.htm.

CHAPTER TEN

1. See the final footnote in Richard Elliott Friedman, *The Bible with Sources Revealed* (San Francisco: HarperOne, 2003), beginning on page 130.
2. The following analysis is based on a lecture entitled "With A Heavy Heart" by Stephen Gabriel Rosenberg of the Institute of Jewish Studies, University College, London, England. See: http://www.biu.ac.il/JH/Parasha/eng/vaera/ros.html.
3. The weighing-of-the-heart ritual was well known in antiquity, well beyond the period of the Exodus. Later in the Bible we are told that the Philistines, sworn enemies of the Israelites, captured their Holy Ark. When the Israelites asked the Philistines to return their ark, they asked them: "Why should you make your hearts heavy—as Egypt and Pharaoh made their hearts heavy?" (1 Samuel 6:6)

   Here, the Israelites clearly equated the evil of the Philistines with the evil of the Egyptians. (Just as Pharaoh would not let the Israelites go, so, too, the Philistines would not let the Holy Ark go.) The phrase "heavy heart"—in its only other biblical use—maintains a unique association with Egyptian evil.
4. Biblical "leprosy" (*tzaraat* in Hebrew) is not the same as the skin disease known today; the word "leprosy" is unfortunately the accepted and only term in English for what the Torah regards as a spiritual disease that has only a spiritual rather than a medical cure. This common misunderstanding has tragically led some to infer sinful behavior in modern-day lepers.

PART III

CHAPTER ELEVEN

1. *Shemesh* in Hebrew is related to *shamash*—the helper-candle used to light the other candles of the menorah on Chanukah. See Rabbi Joseph Telushkin, *Biblical Literacy*, (New York, William Morrow, 1997), 5.
2. The absence of the pronouncement "It was good" on Day 2 is not relevant to our discussion, but it is easily explained when we consider that the creation of water was not completed until Day 3, where "It was good" is mentioned twice—in parallel to Day 6.
3. The table is designed based upon analyses in "Making Sense of the Plagues: The Education of Pharaoh" by Rabbi Yitzchak Etshalom,

posted at www.torah.org/advanced/mikra/5757/sh/dt.57.2.02.html;
Umberto Cassuto, *A Commentary on the Book of Exodus* (Warsaw: Eisen-
brauns, 1967), 93; and Nahum M. Sarna, *Exploring Exodus* (New York:
Schocken, 1996), 76.

4. It is not entirely clear how to translate *veyamesh choshech*, which we
    render (per ArtScroll) as "the darkness will be tangible." Others say the
    darkness will be "palpable" or "the darkness will become darker." In any
    case, the sense of Exodus 10:21 is that of a physically intense darkness
    where Egyptians would essentially be under house arrest, as Exodus
    10:23 informs us: "No man could see his brother nor could anyone rise
    from his place for a three-day period . . ."

5. The first three plagues might have affected the Israelites. It is only at
    this point, beginning with the fourth plague, that we are told that God
    made a distinction between the two peoples.

6. The location is not identified, but where else would Moses go to meet
    the king? Nevertheless, uncertainty as to location does not diminish the
    narrative's consistency since the second plague in each set is consistently
    not stated.

7. Rabbi Elchanan Samet develops this argument. See: www.vbm-torah.
    org/parsha.60/40balak.htm.

8. In a deft literary maneuver, the author employs parallel bookends to
    underscore the main idea. In the first bookend of the story, Balak
    beseeches Balaam's aid, saying, "For I know that whomever you bless
    is blessed and whomever you curse is cursed" (Num. 22:7), as though
    the prophet himself has this power. The parallel bookend comes in
    Balaam's third blessing, when he says of Israel, "Those who bless you
    are blessed and those who curse you are cursed" (Num. 24:9). Balaam's
    utterance, dictated by God, clarifies that a prophet is merely a spokes-
    man for his Boss.

9. If the Bible critics had consulted us, we would have advised them to
    drop P altogether. Both P and E use Elokim, so why not argue that E
    wrote Genesis 1, all of the Ten Plagues story, and Balaam? Then E could
    take credit for the triquad.

CHAPTER TWELVE

1. Note that in breaking up the tenth commandment into two separate
    "do not covet" statements, we are following the actual Torah scroll,
    which leaves a space in between these two statements. Visually, this

makes the parallel between them and the first two commandments easier to understand.

2. Note that this verse, Genesis 4:26, reads as follows: "And as for Seth, to him also a son was born, and he named him (*vayikra et-shemo*) Enosh [meaning "man," sharing the same root as *anshei*—see below]. Then the calling in the Name of Hashem began (*huchal*) to be profaned."

Thus 4 and 4' share a unique linguistic connection. Genesis 6:1–4 reads: "And it came to pass when Man began (*hechel*) to increase upon the ground and daughters were born to them. . . . They were the mighty who, from old, were men of renown [i.e., literally, of [great] name—*anshei hashem*]."

Thus, at the inception of idolatry, which arrives with the naming of Enosh (*shemo Enosh*), we have the start of a process of deterioration (*huchal*); this downward process continued (*hechel*) until the domination of men of renown (*anshei hashem*—which is, roughly, *shemo Enosh* backwards; in other words, this is the opposite of what God wanted from man).

3. Genesis 1 begins with the fivefold repetition of the word "light":

> . . . Elokim said: "Let there be **light**," and there was **light**. Elokim saw that the **light** was good, and Elokim separated between the **light** and the darkness. Elokim called to the **light**—"Day," and to the darkness He called—"Night." And there was evening and there was morning, one day.

Genesis 12, which introduces us to Abram, begins with the fivefold repetition of the word blessing:

> . . . And I will make of you a great nation; I will **bless** you . . . and you shall be a **blessing**. I will **bless** those who **bless** you . . . and all the families of the earth shall **bless** themselves by you.

The light that God introduced at creation (P) did not bring universal blessing to the world; for this reason, God chose a righteous individual, Abraham (J), to spread blessing in the world.

4. The words share the same Hebrew letters: *ayin-resh-vav-mem*.

5. Isaac M. Kikawada and Arthur Quinn, *Before Abraham Was* (Ft. Collins: Ignatius Press, 1989), 104.

6. Based in part on Michael Fishbane, *Biblical Text and Texture: A Literary Reading of Selected Texts* (Oxford: Oneworld Publications, 1998), 42.

CHAPTER THIRTEEN

1. The first of the seven "and it was so" statements is worded slightly differently than the other six, but the function and rhythm are the same. The first mention is *vayehi or*, meaning "and there was light." The other six times we have *vayehi chen*—"and it was so." In each of the seven cases, God spoke and the Creation occurred, so the two variants serve the same function. Also, *vayehi or* and *vayehi chen* have the same number of syllables in Hebrew; therefore each has the same rhythm. The other creations do not have the same number of syllables, so saying "and there was a firmament" would lessen the Torah's literary power. The author does not rigidly follow stilted formulas but selects language that reads and sounds more literary.

2. For more on Leviticus and both voluntary and obligatory offerings, see: Menachem Leibtag's essay, "*Parshat Vayikra*—The *Korban Yachid*: *N'dava* and *Chova*,"—http://www.tanach.org/vayikra/vayik/shiur2.htm.

3. Menachem Leibtag's essay, "*Parshat Tzav*—The Difference Between *Tzav* and *Vayikra*"—http://www.tanach.org/vayikra/tzav.doc—was helpful in clarifying the differences between Leviticus 1–5 and 6–7.

4. This insight comes from one of the many discussions (*sichos*) of the Lubavitcher Rebbe, Menachem Mendel Schneerson.

CHAPTER FOURTEEN

1. We have summarized his theory based on the work of John Rogerson, a respected Bible scholar, and an unabashed admirer of Wellhausen. See: *Old Testament Criticism in the Nineteenth Century: England and Germany* (London: SPCK/Fortress, 1985), 260–264.

2. Wellhausen's entry on Israel in a nineteenth-century volume of the *Encylopedia Britannica* contains a lengthy diatribe against Judaism, which, he says, "takes the soul out of religion and spoils morality." See: Moshe Weinfeld, *Getting at the Roots of Wellhausen's Understanding of the Law of Israel, On the 100th Anniversary of the Prolegomena* (Jerusalem: Institute for Advanced Studies, The Hebrew University, 1979) no. 14: 4–5.

3. A French dilettante, Abbé d'Aubignac, considered the "Father of the Homeric Problem," laid out his ideas in *Conjectures académiques; ou, dis-*

sertation sur l'Iliade. It was published posthumously in 1715, thirty-eight years before Astruc's *Conjectures sur les mémoires originaux dont il parait que Moïse s'est servi pour composer le livre de la Genèse.* Note the similar style of the titles. See: Umberto Cassuto, *The Documentary Hypothesis* (Jerusalem: Shalem Press, 2006), 12.

APPENDIX A

1. Richard Elliott Friedman, *The Bible with Sources Revealed* (San Francisco: HarperOne, 2003), footnote on p. 77.
2. When men call upon the name Hashem righteously, rather than profanely, they do so using the verb *k-r-a*—alone and without *h-ch-l* as an auxiliary. See, for example, Gen. 12:8; Gen. 21:33; Gen. 26:25; and Gen. 33:20.
3. Each of these four sections mentions both land and seed because a nation needs a land, and a land without a nation is useless. But either land or seed is dominant in each section.
4. Friedman, *The Bible with Sources Revealed*, 1.

ACKNOWLEDGMENTS

Writing a book and seeing it through to publication is no small undertaking. Without the help of numerous others, it would be impossible for first-time authors to succeed in such a venture. It is therefore with humility and deep gratitude that we acknowledge the enormous debt owed those who have helped us along the way.

First, we salute our dream publisher Richard Vigilante. Where so many agents and publishers before him saw a risky book by two unknown authors that completely rejected the widely held view of academic experts (one example: "[Name Withheld] didn't even want to take a look at it; she feels there is too much academic evidence to the contrary."), Richard read the book with an open mind, found it convincing, and saw its potential. Moreover, he offered his candid advice on how the book could be improved, and though his suggestions meant that these already exhausted authors would need to make significant revisions, we did so with renewed vigor because we knew he was right.

Although we have included numerous endnotes, readers should not infer from the absence of a bibliography that we have no intellectual debt to account for. The one indispensable source on the authorship of the Bible is the great Italian biblical scholar Umberto Cassuto. He published his work in Italian in the 1930s and in Hebrew in the 1940s, and these books were translated into English in the 1960s. Cassuto clearly and logically demolished the documentary hypothesis long ago, but indefensibly his work was ignored. We recommend his brief work, *The Documentary Hypothesis and the Composition of the Pentateuch: Eight Lectures*. More ambitious readers will be rewarded for consulting his far more extensive findings in *A Commentary on the Book of Genesis I & II and A Commentary on the Book of Exodus*.

Another invaluable source for our book was the extraordinary work of several rabbis all affiliated with Yeshivat Har Etzion, a rabbinical academy in the Gush Etzion region of Israel. It is a testament to the Internet age that the authors have learned so much from people we have never personally met, in particular Rabbi Yoel Bin-Nun, Rabbi Menachem Leibtag, Rabbi Elchanan Samet, Rabbi Yair Kahn, Rabbi Ezra Bick, Rabbi Yonatan Grossman, and Rabbi Yaacov Medan. Readers looking for good current scholarship on the literary composition of the Torah need look no further than the Yeshiva's website: www.vbm-torah.org.

Many of our friends and relations read early drafts of the book and offered valuable criticism and encouragement. We want to thank Jay Nagdeman, Lenny Steiner, David Libo, Ira Siegel, Avremy Chein, Andy Small, Harry Stark, Shelly Bright, Elisabeth Kesten, David Rose, and Michael and Anita Kline. Ken Silber's sharp eye and nuanced reading gave the book its first edit, and Ken Fisher, Jeff Herman, Yitta Halberstam, and Judy Gruen provided crucial help at sensitive times. Rabbi Daniel Lapin kindly placed his distinguished name on our book jacket after reading the final version.

Most importantly, we couldn't have written this book without the love and help of our families, starting with our parents Dr. Zeev and Varda Rav-Noy, and Harriet Weinreich. Eyal thanks his wife Tzippy for her constant encouragement and belief in the project, and Gil thanks his wife Nedra for her uncommon insight and unflagging support.

INDEX